The Role of the International Criminal Court in Preventing Atrocity Crimes through Timely Intervention

The Role of the International Criminal Court in Preventing Atrocity Crimes through Timely Intervention

From the Humanitarian Intervention Doctrine and Ex Post Facto Judicial Institutions to the Notion of Responsibility to Protect and the Preventative Role of the International Criminal Court

Inaugural lecture as Chair in International Criminal Law and International Criminal Procedure at Utrecht University, delivered on 18 October 2010

by

Dr. Hector Olásolo

eleven
international publishing

Published, sold and distributed by Eleven International Publishing
P.O. Box 85576
2508 CG The Hague
The Netherlands
Tel.: +31 70 33 070 33
Fax: +31 70 33 070 30
e-mail: sales@budh.nl
www.elevenpub.com

Sold and distributed in USA and Canada
International Specialized Book Services
920 NE 58th Avenue, Suite 300
Portland, OR 97213-3786, USA
Tel: 1-800-944-6190 (toll-free)
Fax: +1 503 280-8832
orders@isbs.com
www.isbs.com

Eleven International Publishing is an imprint of Boom uitgevers Den Haag.

Cover photograph: ICC-CPI2006_49 031©ICC-CPI Hans Hordijk
Lay-out: Wieneke Matthijsse

ISBN 978-94-90947-40-8

Printed in The Netherlands

Rector Magnificus,[1]

'[T]he brutal legacy of the twentieth century speaks bitterly' of the collective inadequacies of international institutions and 'the profound failure of individual States to live up to their most basic and compelling responsibilities.'[2] Given the profound and long-lasting costs to a society of engaging in atrocity crimes,[3] strengthening preventative action becomes of utmost relevance.[4] This is emphasised by the emerging notion of 'responsibility to protect'.[5] In this inaugural lecture, I will address the role of the International Criminal Court (ICC) in implementing the notion of responsibility to protect through means other than ending impunity for past crimes.

I Humanitarian Intervention Doctrine and Responsibility to Protect

The nineties saw the establishment, by the United Nations (UN), or with the direct involvement of the United Nations, of several international tribunals with jurisdiction over atrocity crimes that had already taken place.[6] These tribunals were characterised by their primacy over national jurisdictions, their temporary nature, and the limitation of their jurisdiction to a specific crisis situation, such as the breakup of the former Yugoslavia or the

---

1 The author thanks Gordon Brandt and Margaret Wichmann for their research on legislation, case law and doctrine. The author is profoundly thankful to dr. Annemarieke Beijer, Wouter de Zanger and Wieneke Matthijsse, colleagues at the Willem Pompe Institute, for their work on the Dutch version of the present inaugural lecture. The views expressed herein are those of the author alone and do not necessarily reflect the views of the ICC, the ICTY, the United Nations in general or the Spanish Government.

2 United Nations General Assembly (UNGA) 'Implementing the Responsibility to Protect: Report of the Secretary-General' (12 Jan 2009) UN Doc A/63/677 paras 5, 6 [hereinafter UNGA, On Responsibility to Protect].

3 In this paper, the term 'atrocity crimes' includes the following crimes: genocide, crimes against humanity including ethnic cleansing, and war crimes. See in this regard, D. Scheffer, 'Atrocity Crimes Framing the Responsibility to Protect' (2007-2008) 40 *Case Western Reserve Journal of International Law* 111, 117 [hereinafter Scheffer, 'Atrocity Crimes']. See also D. Scheffer, 'Genocide and Atrocity Crimes' (2006) 1 *Genocide Studies and Prevention* 229, 238-9.

4 As UNGA, On Responsibility to Protect (Above n. 2) highlights at para 32, '[t]he difference between the two paths can amount to the choice between national potential preserved or destroyed.'

5 UNGA, On Responsibility to Protect (Above n. 2) at p. 2, paras 1-10.

6 A. Cassese, 'From Nuremberg to Rome: International Military Tribunals to the International Criminal Court', in: A. Cassese, A. Eser, G. Gaja, P. Kirsch, A. Pellet and B. Swart (eds.), *The Rome Statute to the International Criminal Court,* vol I (Oxford, Oxford University Press, 2002) 10-7.

Rwandan genocide.[7] As explained by Leila Sadat and Michael Scharf, they were part of a broader post-conflict UN strategy, and their primary goal was to facilitate reconciliation.[8]

Extending the basis for judicial intervention, while perpetuating a global system that tolerated atrocity crimes through inaction, was unsustainable.[9] As a consequence, the nineties also saw the greatest development of the humanitarian intervention doctrine, and its application to situations such as those in Somalia in 1993 and Kosovo in 1999.[10] This doctrine is based on the understanding of sovereignty as responsibility, which can be traced back to Francisco de Vitoria and Bartolomé de las Casas. Their ideas led to the 1542 New Laws of the Indies, which abolished native slavery for the first time in European colonial history.[11] In the early seventeenth century, Jesuit Fran

---

7 R. Cryer, H. Friman, D. Robinson and E. Wilmshurst, *An Introduction to International Criminal Law and Procedure* (Cambridge, Cambridge University Press, 2007) 102-17 [hereinafter Cryer, *An Introduction*].

8 L. Sadat, 'The Legacy of the ICTY: The International Criminal Court' (2003) 37 *New England Law Review* 1073; V. Morris and M. Scharf, *An Insider's Guide to the International Criminal Tribunal for the Former Yugoslavia*, vol. I (Irvington-on-Hudson, Transnational Publishers, 1995) 17-36. See also United Nations Security Council (UNSC) 'Report of the Secretary-General Pursuant to Paragraph 2 of the Security Counsel Resolution 808(1993)' (3 May 1993) UN Doc S/25704; UNSC 'Report of the Secretary-General Pursuant to Paragraph 5 of Security Council Resolution 955 (1994)' (13 Feb 1995) UN Doc S/1995/134.

9 International Commission on Intervention and State Sovereignty (ICISS), *The Responsibility to Protect* (Ottawa, International Development Research Centre, 2001) [hereinafter ICISS, 'Responsibility to Protect']. See also Scheffer, Atrocity Crimes (Above n. 3) at 117.

10 See generally A. Hehir, *Humanitarian Intervention: an Introduction* (London, Palgrave Macmillan, 2010). For a specific account of humanitarian intervention in Kosovo see *ibid* at 201-20. For a specific account of humanitarian intervention in Somalia see F. Teson, *Humanitarian Intervention: An Inquiry into Law and Morality*, 3rd edn (Ardsley, Transnational Publishers, 2005) 298 [hereinafter Teson, *Humanitarian Intervention*].

11 The ideas of Francisco de Vitoria (1483/1486-1546) and Bartolomé de las Casas (1485-1566) led to the approval of the 'New Laws of the Indies for the Good Treatment and Preservation of the Indians'. The New Laws, which abolished native slavery for the first time in European colonial history, were passed to prevent the exploitation of the Indigenous peoples of the Americas by large scale landowners (*Encomenderos*) by strictly limiting their power and dominion. Franciso de Vitoria extrapolated his ideas of legitimate sovereign power to society at the international level. For him, not only relations between states ought to respect the rights of all, but there was also a common good of the world that was superior to the good of each state. As a result, relations between states had to pass from being justified by force to being justified by law and justice. See the translation of those extracts of Vitoria's works *De Indis* (1532) and *De Jure belli Hispanorum in barbaros* (1532) contained in his posthumous work F. de Vitoria and J.B. Scott (ed.), *Relectiones Theologicae* (New York, London, Oceana Publications, 1917). They were reprinted by the Carnegie Institution of Washington in 1964 with the edition of Ernest Nys, who highlighted his influence over Hugo Grotius. See also B. de las Casas and N. Griffin (tr.), *Brevísima relación de la destrucción de las Indias (A Short Account of the Destruction of the Indies)* (London, Penguin Classics, 1999). This is a translated version of the 1542 De las Casas work. After the approval of the 1542 New Laws, a debate concerning the treatment of natives of the Indies was held in the Spanish city of Valladolid in 1550 and 1551. It opposed two main positions. On the one hand, Bartolomé de las Casas, Dominican and Bishop of Chiapas, argued that natives of the Indies were free men in the natural order and deserved the same treatment as others, according to Catholic theology. On the other hand, fellow Dominican Juan Ginés Sepúlveda insisted the Indians were natural slaves, and therefore reducing them to slavery or serfdom was consistent with Catholic theology and natural law. The New Laws were kept after the triumph of De las Casas' position. See

cisco Suarez, leading representative of the School of Salamanca,[12] underscored that political power originates in the consensus of free wills, and that men are thus entitled to disobey even to the point of deposing an unjust government.[13] Subsequently, Hugo Grotius,[14] John Locke,[15] and the contract theorists of the eighteenth century, developed the notion of sovereignty as responsibility so as to shape it into its current form.

Based on this premise, the humanitarian intervention doctrine, formulated for the first time by Hersch Lauterpacht in the immediate aftermath of World War II,[16] justifies a right of armed intervention into a state that is unwilling or unable to protect its own population against atrocity crimes.[17] According

---

A. Losada, *The Controversy between Sepúlveda and Las Casas in the Junta of Valladolid* (DeKalb, Northern Illinois University Press, 1971) 280-2. See also B. Keen, *The Legacy of Bartolomé de Las Casas* (Boulder, Westview Press, 1998) 57-69; D.A. Brading, *The First America: the Spanish Monarchy, Creole Patriots, and the Liberal State 1492-1867* (Cambridge, Cambridge University Press, 1991) 80-8; A. Padgen, *The Fall of Natural Man: The American Indian and the Origins of Comparative Ethnology* (Cambridge, Cambridge University Press, 1982) 109; J. Crow, *The Epic of Latin America*, 4th edn (Berkeley, University of California Press, 1992).

12 The leading members of the School of Salamanca were Francisco de Vitoria (1486-1546), Domingo de Soto (1494-1560), Martín de Azpilicueta (1491-1486), Tomás de Mercado (1525-1575) and Francisco Suarez (1548-1617).

13 See in particular F. Suárez, G.L. Williams and H. Davis (tr.), 'Defensio Fidei Catholicae adversus Anglicanae sectae errores (The Defense of the Catholic Faith against the errors of the Anglican)' (1613), in: F. Suárez, *Selections from three works of Francisco Suárez, S.J.: De legibus, ac deo legislatore, 1612; Defensio fidei catholicae, et apostolicae adversus anglicanae sectae errores, 1613; De triplici virtute theologica, fide, spe, et charitate, 1621* (London, Oxford, Clarendon Press, 1944) 647-728.

14 This understanding is reflected in Grotius' conception of things that are public and common to all men. See H. Grotius and R. Magoffin (tr.), *De Mare Liberum*, (1609) (New York, Oxford University Press 1916) 22-44; H. Grotius and F. Kelsey (tr.), *Dejure Belli AC Pacis* book II (1625) (Gloucestershire, Clarendon Press, 1925) ch 2; see generally H. Lauterpacht, 'The Grotian Tradition in International Law', in: H. Lauterpacht, *British Yearbook of International Law* (London, New York, Toronto, Oxford University Press, 1946) 1, 27.

15 See, for example, J. Locke, 'The Second Treatise of Government' (1690), in: P. Laslet (ed.), *Two Treatises of Government*, 3rd edn (Cambridge, Cambridge University Press, 1988) 265.

16 H. Lauterpacht (ed.), *Oppenheim's International Law: A Treatise*, 6th edn (London, Longmans Green and Company, 1947) 280. See also P. Jessup, *A Modern Law of Nations* (New York, The Macmillan Company, 1948) 172-74; I. Brownlie, 'Humanitarian Intervention', in: J. Moore (ed.), *Law and Civil War in the Modern World* (Baltimore, Johns Hopkins University Press, 1974) 217; I. Brownlie, 'The Principle of Non-Use of Force in Contemporary International Law', in: W. Butler (ed.), *The Non-Use of Force in International Law* (1989) 17.

17 According to its supporters, 'humanitarian intervention [is] the proportionate transboundary help, including forcible help, provided by governments to individuals in another state who are being denied basic human rights and who themselves would be rationally willing to revolt against their oppressive government.' See Teson, *Humanitarian Intervention* (Above n. 10) at 5. See also B.F. Burmester, 'On Humanitarian Intervention: The New World Order and Wars to Preserve Human Rights' (1994) 1 *Utah Law Review* 269; J. Delbruck, 'A Fresh Look at Humanitarian Intervention Under the Authority of the United Nations' (1992) 67 *Indiana Law Journal* 887, 897-901; R. Gordon, 'Humanitarian Intervention by the United Nations: Iraq, Somalia, and Haiti' (1996) 31 *Texas International Law Journal* 43, 44-6; R. Lillich, 'Forcible Self Help Under International Law' (1980) 62 *Readings in International Law from the Naval War College Review* 129, 134; J. Nafziger, 'Self-Determination and Humanitarian Intervention in a Community of Power' (1991) 20 *Denver Journal of International Law and Policy* 9, 21-6. For these authors, humanitarian intervention was not unlawful under article 2(4) of the UN Charter because (i) it does

to its supporters, humanitarian intervention by the United Nations, or by states with or without UN authorisation, is consistent with the principles of sovereignty and territorial integrity embraced in the UN Charter. Such principles, they argued, aim to protect the citizens of states rather than states as entities.[18] As a result, they cannot apply in favour of states that perpetrate or otherwise fail to prevent atrocity crimes.

Nevertheless, the humanitarian intervention doctrine has been progressively abandoned in the last decade for several reasons.[19] First, it failed to provide precise criteria to define those circumstances giving rise to the alleged right to armed intervention.[20] Second, it did not receive broad consensus as many argued that the UN Charter's prohibition on the use of force admits of no exception for humanitarian intervention.[21] Third, as the notion of humanitarian intervention was limited to reaction to actual atrocity crimes, it left states with no other option than to choose between two undesirable

not violate the territorial integrity of a state, since the purpose of such intervention is not to gain territory or alter an existing border; and (ii) it does not violate the political independence of states because it does not seek to subject the recalcitrant state to the political domination of the intervening state. Moreover, it was in consonance with the Charter's goals of promoting human rights and self-determination. See in particular R. Lillich 'Forcible Self-Help by States to Protect Human Rights' (1967) 53 *Iowa Law Review* 325, 332-8 [hereinafter Lillich, 'Forcible Self-Help']; R. Lillich, 'Humanitarian Intervention: A Reply to Ian Brownlie and a Plea for Constructive Alternatives', in: J. Moore (ed.), *Law and Civil War in the Modern World* (Baltimore, Johns Hopkins University Press, 1974) 229 [hereinafter Lillich, 'Humanitarian Intervention']; R. Lillich, 'Intervention to Protect Human Rights' (1969) 15 *McGill Law Journal* 205 [hereinafter Lillich, 'Intervention']; J.N. Moore, 'Toward an Applied Theory for the Regulation of Intervention', in: J.N. Moore (ed.), *Law and Civil War in the Modern World* (Baltimore, Johns Hopkins University Press, 1974) 3, 24-5 [hereinafter Moore, 'Toward']; W. Reisman, 'Sovereignty and Human Rights in Contemporary International Law' (1990) 84 *American Journal of International Law* 866 [hereinafter Reisman, 'Sovereignty'].

18 Lillich, 'Forcible Self-Help' (Above n. 17) at 332-8; Lillich, 'Humanitarian Intervention' (Above n. 17) at 229; Lillich, 'Intervention' (Above n. 17); Moore, 'Toward' (Above n. 17) at 24-5; Reisman, 'Sovereignty' (Above n. 17).

19 The theoretical debates over humanitarian intervention are summarised in S. Murphy, *Humanitarian Intervention: The United Nations in an Evolving World Order* (Washington, DC, PAIL Institute, 1996) 202-12; O. Ramsbotham and T. Woodhouse, *Humanitarian Intervention in Contemporary Conflict: A Reconceptualization* (Cambridge, Polity Press, 1991) 33-65; D. Richemond, 'Normativity in International Law: The Case of Unilateral Humanitarian Intervention' (2003) 6 *Yale Human Rights and Development Law Journal* 45, 48-9.

20 See generally R. Zacklin, 'Beyond Kosovo: the United Nations and Humanitarian Intervention', in: L.C. Vorah, F. Pocar, Y. Fetherstone, O. Fourney, C. Graham, J. Hocking and N. Robson (eds.), *Man's Inhumanity to Man* (The Hague, Kluwer Law International, 2003) 935; T. Franck, 'Legality and Legitimacy in Humanitarian Intervention', in: T. Nardin and M.S. Williams (eds.), *Humanitarian Intervention* (New York, New York University Press, 2006) 143.

21 M. Akehurst, 'Humanitarian Intervention', in: H. Bull (ed.), *World Politics* (Oxford, Clarendon Press, 1984) 95, 104-7; I. Brownlie, *International Law and the Use of Force by States* (Oxford, Claredon Press, 1963) 338-42. See also N. Ronzitti, *Rescuing Nationals Abroad Through Military Coercion and Intervention on Grounds of Humanity* (Dordrecht, Martinus Nijhoff Publishing, 1985).

choices: (i) standing by in the face of mounting civilian deaths; or (ii) deploying military force to protect the threatened populations.[22]

With the loss of support for the humanitarian intervention doctrine and the structural limitations of *ex-post facto* judicial institutions, there was a need to identify new effective mechanisms for preventing atrocity crimes. The notion of responsibility to protect, endorsed by the UN General Assembly at the 2005 World Summit,[23] reaffirmed by the UN Security Council in 2006,[24] and further elaborated on by the UN Secretary-General in 2009, aims at fulfilling this role.[25]

Like the humanitarian intervention doctrine, the notion of responsibility to protect is based on the understanding of sovereignty as responsibility. Nevertheless, it has several distinctive features, which, as Carsten Stahn has pointed out,[26] have secured its broad acceptance in a short period of time. First, it addresses the dilemma of intervention from the perspective of those

22 UNGA, On Responsibility to Protect (Above n. 2) at paras 5-6. Moreover, as highlighted by the ICISS, 'external military intervention for humanitarian protection purposes has been controversial both when it has happened – as in Somalia, Bosnia and Herzegovina and Kosovo – and when it has failed to happen, as in Rwanda.' ICISS, 'Responsibility to Protect' (Above n. 9) at 7.

23 In response to Kofi Annan's question at the 2000 Millennium address, the Canadian Government established an ICISS, which, under the chairmanship of Gareth Evans and Mohamed Sahnoun, left aside the controversial doctrine of humanitarian intervention to focus on the new emerging notion of responsibility to protect. ICISS, 'Responsibility to Protect' (Above n. 9) was issued in December 2001. For an insider account of the work of the Commission and the ideas that shaped it, see G. Evans, *The Responsibility to Protect: Ending Mass Atrocity Crimes Once and for All* (Washington, D.C., Brookings Institution Press, 2008). See also A. Bellamy, *A Responsibility to Protect: the Global Effort to End Mass Atrocities* (Cambridge, Polity Press, 2009); R. Thakur, *The United Nations, Peace and Security: From Collective Security to the Responsibility to Protect* (Cambridge, Cambridge University Press, 2006) 245-86; T. Weiss and D. Hubert, *The Responsibility to Protect: Research, Bibliography and Background* (Ottawa, International Development Research Centre, 2001); R. Thakur, 'Outlook: Intervention, Sovereignty and the Responsibility to Protect Experience from ICISS' (2002) 33 *Security Dialogue* 323. The notion of responsibility to protect was subsequently endorsed by the UN Secretary-General's (UNSG) High-Level Panel on Threats, Challenges and Change (see UNSG's High-Level Panel on Threats, Challenges and Change, 'A more secure world: Our shared responsibility' (2 Dec 2004) UN Doc A/59/565 paras 65-6). On 16 September 2005, the UN General Assembly in the framework of the 2005 World Summit approved, by consensus, the concept of responsibility to protect in relation to atrocity crimes. (UNGA '2005 World Summit Outcome'(24 Oct 2005) UN Doc Res A/Res/60/1 paras 138-9 [hereinafter UNGA Res A/Res/60/1]). The General Assembly adopted the Summit Outcome in its resolution. *Ibid* at para 138.

24 In Paragraph 4 of UNSC Resolution (Res) 1674 (2006) (28 Apr 2006) UN Doc S/RES/1674, on the protection of civilians in armed conflict, the Security Council reaffirmed the provisions of paragraphs 138 and 139 of the Summit Outcome regarding the responsibility to protect populations from genocide, war crimes, ethnic cleansing and crimes against humanity. In the second preambular paragraph of UNSC Res 1706 (2006) (31 Aug 2006) UN Doc S/Res/1706 on the crisis in Darfur, the Council recalled its earlier reaffirmation of those provisions.

25 UNGA, On Responsibility to Protect (Above n. 2). See also C. Joyner, 'The Responsibility to Protect: Humanitarian Concern and the Lawfulness of Armed Intervention' (2007) 47 *Virginia Journal of International Law* 693, 709.

26 C. Stahn, 'Responsibility to Protect: Political Rhetoric or Emerging Legal Norm?' (2007) 101 *The American Journal of International Law* 99, 101, 118.

suffering atrocity crimes rather than from the perspective of those asserting a right to intervention.[27]

Second, it does not limit responsibility and intervention to reaction to actual atrocity crimes. On the contrary, the notion of responsibility to protect constitutes a holistic approach to address crisis situations[28] based on the premise that an effective response requires a continuing intervention that starts with the adoption of preventative measures.[29] Only if such measures fail, reaction to actual atrocity crimes will be needed.[30] Moreover, the determination of the most appropriate mechanisms for reaction, including military intervention, must be driven by the need to subsequently fulfil the commitment to build a long-lasting peace, and promote good governance, rule of law and sustainable development.[31]

Third, the notion of responsibility to protect is based on a complementarity approach with three main Pillars. According to Pillar I, states whose populations may be at risk have the primary responsibility to protect them from the incitement and commission of atrocity crimes.[32] When states concerned are unable to do so because of capacity deficits or lack of territorial control, third states, as well as the international community at large, must support and assist them under Pillar II.[33] If assistance measures are of no use

27 *Ibid.* at 103.

28 The need for a multiphased vision of international engagement became evident during the multidimensional UN peacekeeping of the 1990s. Secretary-General Boutros-Ghali developed a tripartite conception of peacemaking, which distinguished peace-preventative diplomacy, peacemaking and 'post-conflict peace building' in his Agenda for Peace. See UNSG, 'An Agenda for Peace-Preventative Diplomacy, Peacemaking, and Peace-Keeping' (17 Jun 1992) UN Doc A/47/277-S/24111 para 5. Some aspects of this distinction were subsequently developed in other reports. See for instance, the (i) Brahimi Report, which emphasised the continuous engagement from preventive action to peace building (UNGA and UNSC 'Report of the Panel on United Nations Peace Operations' (21 Aug 2000) UN Doc A/55/305-S/2000/809), and (ii) the 2001 UN Secretary General Report 'No Exit without Strategy', which put the emphasis on post-intervention responsibility (UNSC 'No Exit without strategy: Security Council decision-making and the closure or transition of United Nations peacekeeping operations' (20 Apr 2001) UN Doc. S/2001/394 para 26).

29 UNGA, On Responsibility to Protect (Above n. 2) at paras 1-10.

30 *Ibid.*

31 *Ibid.*

32 See UNGA, Res A/Res/60/1(Above n. 23) at para 138: 'Each individual State has the responsibility to protect its populations from genocide, war crimes, ethnic cleansing and crimes against humanity. This responsibility entails the prevention of such crimes, including their incitement, through appropriate and necessary means. We [States] accept that responsibility and will act in accordance with it.' As UNGA, On Responsibility to Protect (Above n. 2) at para 18 has explained, Pillar I rests on long-standing obligations under international law, according to which responsibility for the prevention of violations of human rights lies with the national protection system of each state. See also N. Jayawickrama, *The Judicial Application of Human Rights Law: National, Regional and International Jurisprudence* (Cambridge, Cambridge University Press, 2003) 46-50; B. Ramcharan, 'The National Responsibility to Protect Human Rights' (2009) 39 *Hong Kong Law Journal* 361, 369-74.

33 See UNGA Res A/Res/60/1(Above n. 23) at para 139: (i) We [States] also intend to commit ourselves, as necessary and appropriate, to helping States build capacity to protect their populations from genocide, war crimes, ethnic cleansing and crimes against humanity and to assisting

because of the unwillingness of national leadership or the great deficit of national capacity, responsibility devolves to the international community to take timely and decisive action under Pillar III,[34] including armed intervention in extreme circumstances.[35]

As a result, the notion of responsibility to protect can be said to place a particular emphasis on prevention.[36] This has led, in turn, to a shift in the focus of the debate from the criteria under which military intervention, with or without UN authorisation, may be justified, or even required, to the timely implementation of effective preventative measures.

II The Two Dimensions of the ICC's Preventative Mandate: General Prevention and Timely Intervention

As the 21st century has witnessed a change in focus from the humanitarian intervention doctrine to the notion of responsibility to protect, it has also experienced a shift from *ex post facto* judicial institutions to the establishment and consolidation of a permanent International Criminal Court. As Cherif Bassiouni has underlined,[37] the ICC represents a rather different approach to the adjudication of atrocity crimes because it: (i) has been created through an international treaty by the States Parties; (ii) constitutes an independent international organisation with a permanent nature[38]; and (iii) is not part of a broader post-conflict UN strategy.[39]

those which are under stress before crises and conflicts break out.'; and (ii) 'The international community, through the United Nations, also has the responsibility to use appropriate diplomatic, humanitarian and other peaceful means, in accordance with Chapters VI and VIII of the Charter, to help to protect populations from genocide, war crimes, ethnic cleansing and crimes against humanity.' Moreover, according to paragraph 140 of the same resolution: 'We [States] fully support the mission of the Special Adviser of the Secretary-General on the Prevention of Genocide.'

34 UNGA Res A/Res/60/1(Above n. 23) at para 139: 'In this context, we are prepared to take collective action, in a timely and decisive manner, through the Security Council, in accordance with the Charter, including Chapter VII, on a case-by-case basis and in cooperation with relevant regional organizations as appropriate, should peaceful means be inadequate and national authorities are manifestly failing to protect their populations from genocide, war crimes, ethnic cleansing and crimes against humanity.'

35 UNGA, On Responsibility to Protect (Above n. 2) at 40, 50, 56.

36 *Ibid.* at 1-2.

37 M.C. Bassiouni, 'The Making of the International Criminal Court', in: M.C. Bassiouni (ed.), *International Criminal Law* vol 3, 3rd edn (Leiden, Martinus Nijhoff Publishers, 2008) 117-53.

38 UNGA 'Rome Statute of the International Criminal Court' (17 Jul 1998) UN Doc A/Conf.183/9 arts 1, 4 [hereinafter ICC Statute].

39 The ICC has its own political and financial organs, which include an Assembly of States Parties, as well as a Bureau and a Secretariat of the Assembly, and a Budget and Finance Committee (See art 112 ICC Statute; Assembly of States Parties, 'ICC Financial Regulations and Rules,' ICC-ASP/7/5 (21 Nov 2008). Moreover, as provided for in art. 4 ICC Statute, it has international legal personality, and the necessary legal capacity for the exercise of its functions and the fulfilment of its purposes.

In particular, the ICC has been established with a view to act over situations of atrocity crimes that take place after 1st July 2002[40] in the territory of any of its 114 States Parties,[41] and even outside such territory when there is a substantial involvement of their nationals[42] or a UN Security Council's referral.[43] Furthermore, the ICC operates on the basis of a complementarity regime, according to which it can only exercise its jurisdiction when states are inactive, or are unwilling or unable to genuinely carry out their own national proceedings.[44]

There is a clear connection between the notion of responsibility to protect and the ICC's mandate as both have their focus on future situations of atrocity crimes,[45] and are based on the primary responsibility of the states concerned. Indeed, last year, UN Secretary-General Ban Ki-moon referred to the ICC Statute as 'one of the key instruments relating to the responsibility to protect.'[46]

In this regard, it must be noted that the ICC shares with *ex post* facto judicial institutions a commitment to ending impunity as a means to promote: (i) positive general prevention, consisting of upholding the application of international criminal law and reinforcing the core societal values protected therein; and (ii) negative general prevention or deterrence, resulting from sending the message to the world's leadership that those engaging in atrocity crimes will not get away with them.[47] Such commitment is fulfilled by combining judicial proceedings with a number of external relations, outreach and public information activities.[48] The ICC's efforts on general prevention may assist UN officials and other stakeholders to emphasise, under Pillars II and III of the notion of responsibility to protect, both the costs of engaging in atrocity crimes and the benefits of abandonment.[49]

Nevertheless, unlike *ex post facto* judicial institutions, the ICC's preventative mandate has a second dimension. It consists of timely intervention into

40 See art. 11 ICC Statute.

41 See art. 12 ICC Statute.

42 See art. 12 ICC Statute.

43 See arts. 12, 13 (b) ICC Statute.

44 See Para 10 of the Preamble ICC Statute; arts 1, 17 ICC Statute. See also *Situation in the Democratic Republic of the Congo* (Judgment on the Appeal of Mr. Germain Katanga against the Oral Decision of Trial Chamber II of 12 June 2009 on the Admissibility of the Case) ICC-01/04-01/07 0A 8 (25 Sep 2009).

45 The notion of responsibility to protect is confined to four specific crimes (genocide, crimes against humanity, war crimes and ethnic cleansing), which, along with the crime of aggression, also constitute the jurisdiction *ratione materiae* of the ICC (Art. 5 ICC Statute). Nevertheless, it is important to highlight that the International Commission on Intervention and State Sovereignty envisioned the notion of responsibility to protect as having a significantly wider scope (See ICISS, 'Responsibility to Protect' (Above n. 9)). On the controversy about the potential for a wider scope for the notion of responsibility to protect, see Scheffer, 'Atrocity Crimes' (Above n. 3) at 113-6.

46 UNGA, On Responsibility to Protect (Above n. 2), at para 19.

47 Cryer, *An Introduction* (Above n. 7) at 22-39.

48 ICC, 'Outreach',< www.icc-cpi.int/Menus/ICC/Structure+of+the+Court/Outreach>.

49 UNGA, On Responsibility to Protect (Above n. 2) at paras 19, 53.

situations where there are tangible threats of future atrocity crimes, or where atrocity crimes are already taking place. It is mainly discharged by the ICC Prosecutor through his preliminary examinations and investigations, and may cover a broad range of situations as shown by: (i) the 9000 communications received to-date by the Prosecutor from individuals located in more than 140 countries;[50] and (ii) the variety of geographical locations in which preliminary examinations or investigations have been started since 2003: Afghanistan, Central African Republic, Colombia, Darfur, Democratic Republic of Congo, Georgia, Guinea, Iraq, Ivory Coast, Kenya, Palestine, Uganda and Venezuela.[51]

As the notion of responsibility to protect places the emphasis on prevention through timely intervention, the ICC's timely intervention can make a unique contribution to discharging the responsibility of the international community under Pillars II and III of the said notion.

III The ICC's Timely Intervention as a result of Tangible Threats of Future Atrocity Crimes

Atrocity crimes are not unavoidable. They take long planning and preparation, as they require a 'collective effort' and an 'organisational context'.[52] Moreover, there is usually sufficient information about impending atrocity crimes, which, regrettably, is ignored or minimised by high-level national and international decision makers with competing political agendas.[53] Hence, statutory provisions on planning, preparation, incitement and attempt are of the utmost relevance for the effectiveness of preventative efforts through timely intervention. It may thus come as no surprise that, except for the definition of genocide which has always been taken *verbatim* from the 1948 Genocide Convention,[54] the approach taken by the ICC Statute is rather

50 To date the ICC Prosecutor has received 8733 individual communications. See ICC, 'Communications, Referrals, and Preliminary Examinations' <www.icc-cpi.int/Menus/ICC/Structure+of+the+Court/Office+of+the+Prosecutor/ Comm+and+Ref/Communications+and+Referrals.htm>.

51 *Ibid.*

52 K Ambos, 'Epilogue: Future Developments of International Criminal Law in relation to the Responsibility of Superiors for International Crimes', in: H. Olásolo, *The Criminal Responsibility of Senior Political and Military Leaders as Principals to International Crimes* (London, Hart Publishers, 2009) 333.

53 UNGA, On Responsibility to Protect (Above n. 2) at para 6.

54 Genocide is the only exception as its definition, including the references to conspiracy, incitement and attempt, has been taken *verbatim* by the statutes of *ex post facto* judicial institutions, such as the ICTY, the ICTR and the Special Court for Sierra Leone, from the language of the 1948 Convention for the Prevention and Punishment of the Crime of Genocide, which expressly criminalises in its article 3 conspiracy to commit genocide, direct and public incitement to commit genocide and attempt to commit genocide. See also J. Ohlin, 'Attempt to Commit Genocide', in: P. Gaeta (ed.), *The UN Genocide Convention: A Commentary* (Oxford, Oxford University Press, 2009) 183 [hereinafter Ohlin, 'Attempt']; A. Eser, 'Individual Criminal Responsibility', in:

different than that taken by the statutes of the ex post facto judicial institutions. In the latter, as William Schabas has explained, provisions on planning, preparation, incitement and attempt would simply have been superfluous and were not included.[55]

Article 25 of the ICC Statute provides for liability for attempt in relation to all atrocity crimes (not just genocide), and attaches such liability to 'action that commences the execution of a crime by means of a substantial step'.[56] Although this definition requires more than just planning, the question arises as to where to draw the line between mere preparatory acts, and conduct amounting to a substantial step for the execution of atrocity crimes.[57] Neither the ICC Statute nor the case law of international tribunals provide guidance on this matter.[58] Some national systems, such as Germany's, have taken a more restrictive approach and require a direct movement towards the completion of the crime.[59] Others, such as the United States' (US), favour a broader conception by attaching liability for attempt to the possession, collection or fabrication of the means of the crime or the tracking of the victims of the crime.[60]

As a result, should the ICC case law embrace a less restrictive approach, liability for attempt may encompass situations such as that which occurred in Rwanda, where for sixteen consecutive months starting in January 1993, more than half a million machetes were imported and distributed, along with firearms and grenades, under the guise of a self-defence programme.[61]

Article 25 of the ICC Statute also attaches criminal liability to acts of 'public and direct incitement to commit genocide'.[62] Despite its limitation to the crime of genocide, its scope of application may be significant in situations like that in Rwanda where, starting in 1991, the media systematically

---

A. Cassese, P. Gaeta, J.R.W.D. Jones (eds.), *Rome Statute of the International Criminal Court: A Commentary,* vol I (Oxford, Oxford University Press, 2002) 807 [hereinafter Eser, 'Individual']; K. Ambos, 'Article 25 Individual Criminal Responsibility', in: O. Triffterer (ed.), *Commentary on the Rome Statute of the International Criminal Court,* 2nd edn (Oxford, Munich, Hart Publishing and Verlag CH Beck, 2008) 764 [hereinafter Ambos, 'Individual Criminal Responsibility'].

55 W.A. Schabas, *Genocide in International Law* (Cambridge, Cambridge University Press, 2000) 281 [hereinafter Schabas, *Genocide*].

56 See art. 25 (3) (f) ICC Statute.

57 Ohlin, 'Attempt' (Above n. 54) at 178.

58 *Ibid.* at 178, 182-4.

59 See StGB § 22 (Germany). See also Eser, 'Individual' (Above note 54) at 812.

60 See United States Model Penal Code § 5.01(1)(c). See also G.P. Fletcher, *Rethinking Criminal Law*, 2nd edn (New York, Oxford University Press, 2000) 180.

61 *Prosecutor v. Nahimana et al.* (Judgement and Sentence) ICTR-99-52-T (3 Dec 2003) para 113.

62 Regardless of whether genocide actually takes place. See in this regard *Prosecutor v. Akayesu* (Judgement) ICTR-96-4-T (2 Sep 1998) para 561. See also J. Ohlin, 'Incitement and Conspiracy to Commit Genocide', in: P. Gaeta (ed.), *The UN Genocide Convention: A Commentary* (Oxford, Oxford University Press, 2009) 192-5. See in particular art. 25 (3)(e) ICC Statute. In this particular area, the ICC Statute is somewhat more restrictive than the Genocide Convention, as well as than the statutes of the other international and internationalised courts and tribunals, which, although limited to the crime of genocide, provided the notion of 'conspiracy'.

incited Hutus to perpetrate violence against Tutsis,[63] or like that in Cambodia, where for years, the radio of the Khmer Rouge urged listeners to 'purify' the 'masses of the people' of Cambodia.[64]

With regards to the crime of aggression, the definition approved in June 2010 at the first ICC Review Conference, attaches criminal liability to the 'planning' and 'preparation' of an act of aggression.[65] This brings the ICC Statute more in line with most national systems, in which criminal liability can arise as a result of agreeing to commit a crime, participating in the design of a criminal plan or contributing to establish the necessary conditions for its execution.[66] Indeed, if today it is broadly accepted at the national level that criminal liability arises for such preparatory acts, there is no justification to say otherwise at the international level in relation to offences of the magnitude and gravity of atrocity crimes.[67]

Although the existing provisions on attempt and incitement provide a sufficient basis for the ICC's timely intervention, extending liability for

63 *Prosecutor v. Nahimana et al* (Judgement) ICTR-99-52-A (28 Nov 2007) paras 41, 45. See also J.P. Chrétien, *Rwanda: Les Medias du Génocide*, 2nd edn (Paris, Karthala/Reporters sans Frontiers, 2002). In particular, despite several reports during those critical months by the United Nations Assistance Mission in Rwanda and the Special Rapporteur on extrajudicial, arbitrary or summary executions on the incendiary programming of Radio *des Mille Collines*, there was no attempt by the international community to jam such broadcasts. See the UNSC, 'Report of the Secretary-General on the Situation in Rwanda' (31 May 1994) UN Doc S/1994/640 para 11; UNSG, 'Letter Dated 15 December 1999 From the Secretary-General addressed to the President of the Security Council' (16 Dec 1999) UN Doc S/1999/1257, enclosure, annex I; UN Commission for Human Rights, 'Report of the Special Rapporteur on Extrajudicial, Arbitrary or Summary Executions, Mr B.W. Ndiaye, on his Mission to Rwanda from 8 to 17 April 1993' (11 Aug 1993) E/CN.4/1994/7/Add.1.

64 British Broadcasting Corporation, 'Summary of World Broadcasts' FE/5813/A3/2 (15 May 1978).

65 See Assembly of States Parties, 'Amendments to the Rome Statute of the International Criminal Court' Resolution RC/Res. 6 (11 Jun 2010) Annex I, art. 8 bis, para 1.

66 The extension of the scope of criminal law at the national level to criminalise this type of conduct, regardless of whether the commission of the crime is subsequently completed or even started, has been, to an important extent, utilised to confront situations in which a plurality of persons acting in a concerted manner resort systematically to criminal conduct to achieve economic goals (e.g. trafficking of human beings, drugs, weapons, money laundry) or political goals (e.g. terrorism). As a result, it may come as no surprise that national jurisdictions have also extended the criminalisation of preparatory acts to atrocity crimes, which, in addition to constituting the most egregious attacks on the core societal values of the international community, are of a 'unique magnitude', have a 'collective nature' and take place in an 'organisational context'.

67 See on this point the different approaches taken by Cassese and Fletcher on this point in relation to conspiracy to commit genocide: A. Cassese, 'Jurisdiction *ratione materiae*—Genocide', in: A. Cassese, P. Gaeta, and J.R.W.D. Jones (eds.), *The Rome Statute of the International Criminal Court: A Commentary* (Oxford, Oxford University Press, 2002) 347; G.P. Fletcher, 'Amicus Curiae Brief of Specialists in Conspiracy and International Law in Support of Petitioner' 2006 West Law 53979, filed in *Hamdan v. Rumsfeld*, 548 U.S. 557 (2006) 12. Moreover, according to Schabas the exclusion of conspiracy to commit genocide from the Rome Statute was due to 'an oversight of exhausted drafters' (Schabas, *Genocide* (Above n. 55) at 264).

'planning' and 'preparation' to all atrocity crimes will significantly strengthen the ICC's preventative role.[68]

Moreover, as senior leaders are usually directly involved in the planning and preparation of atrocity crimes,[69] focusing on this early stage of the *iter criminis* will reduce the controversy over some forms of criminal liability underscored by Kai Ambos,[70] George Fletcher,[71] Göran Sluiter,[72] Herman van der Wilt,[73] Elise van Sliedregt,[74] Tomas Weigend,[75] or Gerard Werle.[76]

Furthermore, this will be in line with the ICC's gravity threshold, and Luis Moreno-Ocampo's policy of focusing on the 'most responsible persons'.[77]

As long as an individual communication[78] or a referral letter[79] contains tangible *indicia* of attempt or incitement to commit atrocity crimes, the ICC

---

68 In particular, the exclusion of the notion of conspiracy from the realm of art. 25(3) ICC Statute (including in relation to the crime of genocide) appears to be unjustified, particularly in light of its broad acceptance in national legal systems for lesser crimes. The *rationale* for the criminalisation of the notion of conspiracy is that the design of a common plan to commit a serious offence by two or more individuals seriously increases the risk of harming the societal value which is affected when the relevant offence is committed. This risk is further increased when those who have designed the plan to commit the offence begin taking the first steps towards preparing to implement their criminal plan. Logically, the higher the hierarchical position of those involved in the planning of the crime, the higher the level of risk will be. Likewise, the more egregious an attack on a core societal value is, the more legitimate an intervention at an earlier stage of the *iter criminis* in order to prevent the commission of the crime will be. As a result, it appears that the notion of conspiracy is particularly well-suited to prevent the actual completion of atrocity crimes (the most serious crimes of international concern) by senior political and military leaders. In light of these circumstances, and considering the inclusion of conspiracy in the Genocide Convention, in the statutes of the *ad hoc* tribunals and in national jurisdictions, its exclusion from the ICC appears to be unjustified. This is more so if we consider that the definition of the crime of aggression, approved in June 2010 at the first ICC Review Conference, includes the criminalisation of conspiracy-like preparatory acts, such as 'planning'.

69 This situation is normally accompanied by the conscious acquiescence of another sector of the leadership, which refrains from active involvement but does not take the measures within their power to stop such plans and/or preparations.

70 K. Ambos, 'Joint Criminal Enterprise and Command Responsibility' (2007) 5 *Journal of International Criminal Justice* 159, 167-76.

71 G. Fletcher and J. Ohlin, 'Reclaiming Fundamental Principles of Criminal Law in the Darfur Case' (2005) 3 *Journal of International Criminal Justice* 539.

72 A. Zahar and G. Sluiter *International Criminal Law: A Critical Introduction* (Oxford, Oxford University Press, 2007) 221-57.

73 H. van der Wilt, 'Joint Criminal Enterprise Possibilities and Limitations' (2007) 5 *Journal of International Criminal Justice* 91.

74 E. van Sliedregt, 'Joint Criminal Enterprise as a Pathway to Convicting Individuals for Genocide' (2007) 5 *Journal of International Criminal Justice* 184.

75 T. Weigend, 'Intent, Mistake of Law and Co-Perpetration in the *Lubanga* Decision on Confirmation of Charges' (2008) 6 *Journal of International Criminal Justice* 471.

76 G. Werle, 'Individual Criminal Responsibility in Article 25 ICC Statute' (2007) 5 *Journal of International Criminal Justice* 953.

77 See ICC Office of the Prosecutor, 'Paper on Some Policy Issues before the Office of the Prosecutor' (Sep 2003) <www.icc-cpi.int/NR/rdonlyres/1FA7C4C6-DE5F-42B7-8B25-60AA962ED8B6/143594/030905_Policy_Paper.pdf>.

78 See arts 13(c), 15(1) ICC Statute.

79 See arts 13(a) and (b), 14, 53(1) ICC Statute.

Prosecutor must initiate a preliminary examination.[80] This examination aims to distinguish between (i) those situations that require a formal investigation, and (ii) those other situations better dealt with by other means.[81] To make such a determination, it is not sufficient to gather and analyse information concerning the allegations of attempt or incitement. It is also necessary to review the available information regarding *inter alia:* (i) the admissibility of the relevant situation, due to the inaction, unwillingness or inability of national authorities and the gravity of the violence; and (ii) the possible existence of substantial reasons to believe that the investigation would not serve the interests of justice.[82]

As a result, as Antonio Cassese[83] and David Scheffer[84] have pointed out, the Prosecutor can respond appropriately on grounds of admissibility or interest of justice where national authorities take meaningful steps to actually prevent atrocity crimes. Moreover, according to article 25 of the ICC Statute those who start the execution of atrocity crimes by means of a substantial step shall not be liable if they abandon their efforts to commit such crimes or otherwise prevent their completion.[85] Hence, the Prosecutor can close a preliminary examination into allegations of attempt or incitement if his timely intervention has contributed to successfully defusing the threat of atrocity crimes occurring.

---

80 Not only all natural and legal persons have been granted the right to access the ICC by way of individual communications and, in the case of States Parties and the Security Council, referral letters, but they have also been granted the right to be informed of the reasons why the ICC Prosecutor does not intend to proceed with an investigation. See arts 15(6), 53(3) ICC Statute and Rules 104 and 105 of the Rules of Procedure and Evidence. See also H. Olásolo, *The Triggering Procedure of the International Criminal Court* (The Hague, Martinus Nijhoff Publishers, 2005) 65-70 [hereinafter Olásolo, *Triggering Procedure*]

81 Olásolo, *Triggering Procedure* (Above n. 80) at 39-47. See also ICC Presidency, 'Regulations of the Office of the Prosecutor' ICC-BD/05-01-09 (23 Apr 2009), regulations 25-9.

82 According to arts 15(3) and (4), 53(1) ICC Statute, and Rule 48 of the Rules of Procedure and Evidence, these are the different elements of the standard '*reasonable basis* to initiate an investigation', which must be met for the ICC to initiate a formal investigation into a situation. This was underscored in the recent decision of Pre-Trial Chamber II in the relation to the Kenya situation. *Situation in the Republic of Kenya* (Decision Pursuant to Article15 of the Rome Statute on the Authorization of an Investigation into the Situation in the Republic of Kenya) ICC-01/09-19 (31 Mar 2010) paras 26-35.

83 A. Cassese, *International Criminal Law* (Oxford, Oxford University Press, 2008) 395-409.

84 D. Scheffer and A. Cox, 'The Constitutionality of the Rome Statute of the International Criminal Court' (2008) 98 *Journal of Criminal Law and Criminology* 983-1068.

85 According to art. 25(3)(f) ICC Statute: 'Attempts to commit such a crime by taking action that commences its execution by means of a substantial step, but the crime does not occur because of circumstances independent of the person's intentions. However, a person who abandons the effort to commit the crime or otherwise prevents the completion of the crime shall not be liable for punishment under this Statute for the attempt to commit that crime if that person completely and voluntarily gave up the criminal purpose.' See Ambos, 'Individual Criminal Responsibility' (above n. 54) at 764. See also Ohlin, 'Attempt' (Above n. 54), at 175-7.

Although the Prosecutor cannot rely at this stage on measures of a coercive nature,[86] and not all forms of States Party cooperation are available,[87] the potential of preliminary examinations to incentivise national authorities should not be underestimated. As shown by several preliminary examinations, including Georgia,[88] Guinea,[89] and Palestine,[90] the Prosecutor, in addition to receiving testimony and seeking information from reliable sources,[91] may: (i) send missions to the relevant states; (ii) receive in The Hague national delegations of members of governments, representatives of high-courts, opposition leaders and NGOs; (iii) provide advice on those measures that should be taken at the national level to defuse the threat of atrocity crimes; (iv) discuss a prevention strategy with the United Nations and other stakeholders; (v) exchange information with national and inter-

86 Upon the initiation of an investigation, the Prosecutor can also rely on measures of a coercive nature, as well as on all forms of State Party cooperation provided for in Article 93 of the ICC Statute. See arts 54, 57, 93 ICC Statute. Disguising an article 54 ICC Statute investigation as an article 15(2) ICC Statute preliminary examination would be contrary to the limited scope of the latter. See Olásolo, *Triggering Procedure* (Above n. 80) at 59. A different opinion is held by M. Bergsmo and J. Pejic, 'Article 15', in: O. Triffterer (ed.), *Commentary on the Rome Statute of the International Criminal Court*, 2nd edn (Oxford, Munich, Hart Publishing and Verlag CH Beck, 2008) 366.

87 Those forms of State Party cooperation provided for in Article 93 RS in which the Prosecution can rely on at this stage are: (i) the identification and location of persons or items; (ii) the voluntary questioning of victims and witnesses in the territory of the States Parties; (iii) the service of documents, including judicial documents; (iv) the provision of records and documents, including official records and documents; (v) the examination of places or sites; and (vi) any other type of assistance not of a coercive nature which is not prohibited by the law of the requested Statute. See Olásolo, *Triggering Procedure* (Above n. 80) at 60.

88 In relation to the preliminary examination of the situation in Georgia, since the Prosecutor made its preliminary examination public on 14 August 2008, the Georgian Minister of Justice visited the Prosecutor in the Hague; Russia, a State not Party to the Statute, sent to the Prosecutor 3,817 communications, the Prosecutor requested information from the Governments of Russia and Georgia on 27 August 2008, and both of them responded; and two on-site visits have been conducted in Georgia in November 2008 and June 2010, and one in Russia in March 2010. See ICC Office of the Prosecutor, 'Georgia' <www.icc-cpi.int/Menus/ICC/Structure+of+the+Court/Office+of+the+Prosecutor/Comm+And+Ref/Georgia/>.

89 In relation to the preliminary examination of the situation in Guinea, since the Prosecutor made public its preliminary examination on 14 October 2009, consultations were held in January 2010 with President Compaore of Burkina Faso (mediator for the contact group on Guinea) and President Wade of Senegal to ensure that they are informed of Prosecutor's work; two on-sites visits to Guinea have taken place in February and May 2010 to meet *inter lia* with the Guinean Minister of Justice, Colonel Lohalamou, and the Guinean judges took place on 19-21 May 2010. See ICC Office of the Prosecutor, 'Guinea' <www.icc-cpi.int/Menus/ICC/Structure+of+the+Court/Office+of+the+Prosecutor/Comm+and+Ref/Guinea/>.

90 With regard to the preliminary examination of the Palestine situation, a delegation from the Palestinian National Authority, and Representatives of the Arab League visited the Prosecutor on 15 and 16 October 2009, and on 11 January 2010. See ICC Office of the Prosecutor, 'Palestine' <www.icc-cpi.int/Menus/ICC/Structure+of+the+Court/Office+of+the+Prosecutor/Comm+and+Ref/Palestine/>.

91 Art. 15(2) ICC Statute; Rules 104, 105 of the Rules of Procedure and Evidence.

national actors; and (vi) address in the media the evolution of events and the degree of cooperation by national authorities.[92]

Using diplomatic and media channels to bring the world's attention to the plans of senior leaders to engage in atrocity crimes, along with highlighting the possibility of them escaping ICC prosecution should they abandon their plans and take the necessary preventative measures, can be a powerful tool. Moreover, from the perspective of ensuring a timely reaction to tangible threats of atrocity crimes, the ICC Statute appears to offer unprecedented opportunities. While other organs of the international community, such as the UN Security Council or the UN General Assembly, usually require long negotiations before deciding to intervene in a situation, the ICC Prosecutor need not consult with interested stakeholders prior to opening a preliminary examination.

Despite the absence of conclusive evidence at this stage, it appears that the preliminary examination in Afghanistan, contributed to NATO (and in particular the United States) subsequently tightening its airstrike policy.[93] The United States also appears to have reaffirmed its commitment to its internal mechanisms of investigation and prosecution,[94] which may have led to the opening in April 2010 of a high profile military inquiry into civilian deaths allegedly caused by US Special Forces.[95]

In turn, the preliminary examination in Iraq, which started upon the receipt of numerous individual communications since 2003, was closed in light of the proceedings initiated in the United Kingdom with regard to each instance of war crimes allegedly involving British nationals.[96]

Moreover, the preliminary examination in Kenya appears to have strengthened the message sent by former UN Secretary-General Kofi Annan

92 See in this regard, W. Burke-White, 'Implementing a Policy of Positive Complementarity in the Rome System of Justice' (2008) 19 *Criminal Law Forum* 59, 61 [hereinafter Burke-White, 'Implementing']; C. Hall, 'Developing and Implementing an Effective Positive Complementarity Prosecution Strategy', in: C. Stahn and G. Sluiter, *The Emerging Practice of the International Criminal Court* (Leiden, Brill, 2009) 220 [hereinafter Hall, 'Developing'].

93 D. Schwammenthal, 'Prosecuting American 'War Crimes'' *The Wall Street Journal* (The Hague, 26 Nov 2009) Opinion Europe. See also D. Filkins, 'U.S. Tightens Airstrike Policy in Afghanistan' *The New York Times* (21 Jun 2009) Asia Pacific.

94 See E. Barbour and M.C. Weed, 'The International Criminal Court (ICC): Jurisdiction, Extradition, and U.S. Policy' (Congressional Research Service 16 Mar 2010) <assets.opencrs.com/rpts/R41116_20100316.pdf>, 15.

95 See L. King, 'Inquiry puts Spotlight on U.S. Special Forces in Afghanistan' *The Los Angeles Times* (9 Apr 2010) referring to the high profile inquiry into alleged civilian deaths caused by special forces who, until then, had been largely shielded from the public spotlight which was opened by the US military in April 2010.

96 ICC Office of the Prosecutor, 'OTP Response to communications received concerning Iraq' (9 Feb 2010) <www.icc-cpi.int/NR/rdonlyres/04D143C8-19FB-466C-AB77-4CDB2FDEBEF7/143682/OTP_letter_to_senders_re_Iraq_9_February_2006.pdf>, 9.

to caution Kenyan authorities that there will be no impunity for those engaging in atrocity crimes.[97]

Whenever a preliminary examination is unsuccessful in incentivising national authorities, the investigation stage,[98] in which the Prosecutor can rely on coercive measures[99] and all forms of State Party cooperation, may prove to be a useful mechanism to fulfil the ICC's preventative mandate. Article 53 of the ICC Statute empowers the Prosecutor to close an investigation when 'there is no sufficient basis for a prosecution'. This standard is comprised of similar criteria to those applicable during the preliminary examination.[100] As a result, the Prosecutor can close an investigation if it has served to prompt reluctant national authorities to take meaningful steps to actually prevent the commission of atrocity crimes.[101]

IV The ICC's Timely Intervention When Atrocity Crimes Are Already Taking Place

The ICC's timely intervention can also take place in situations in which atrocity crimes are already occurring. The focus in these situations will be on stopping ongoing atrocity crimes.

Moreover, abandonment of future crimes will not exclude liability for those already committed. Therefore, preliminary examinations and investigations could only be brought to an end by the Prosecutor on admissibility or interest of justice grounds.

97 See the research paper by C. Bjork and J. Goebertus, from Harvard Law School, 'Parallel Paths and Unintended Consequences: The Role of Civil Society and the ICC in Rule of Law Strengthening in Kenya' (forthcoming) works.bepress.com/christine_bjork/1/. See also Kofi Annan Foundation, 'Remarks by Kofi Annan on Conclusion of the Visit to Kenya, 2-8 December 2009' (Press Release Dec 2009) <kofiannanfoundation.org/newsroom/press/2009/12/remarks-he-kofi-annan-conclusion-visit-to-kenya-au-panel-eminent-african>. Nevertheless, far more empirical research is necessary to have more certainty about the impact of the Preliminary Examination of the ICC.

98 In this cases, a qualitative approach to the gravity threshold may still justify the start of an investigation into a situation where atrocity crimes have not been yet committed, or are starting being committed. For a definition of a qualitative approach to the gravity threshold see *Prosecutor v. Abu Garda* (Decision on the Confirmation of Charges) ICC-02/05-02/09 (8 Feb 2010) paras 31-3; *Situation in the Republic of Kenya* (Decision Pursuant to Article 15 of the Rome Statute on the Authorization of an Investigation into the Situation in the Republic of Kenya) ICC-01/09 (31 Mar 2010) para 62.

99 See arts 54-7 ICC Statute.

100 Compare art. 53 (2) ICC Statute with art. 53 (1) ICC Statute and rule 48 of the ICC Rules of Procedure and Evidence.

101 Moreover, under article 19, paragraph 11, of the ICC Statute, the Prosecutor may decide to suspend his investigation and monitor the development of events at the national level prior to formally close it.

In this context, prompting national authorities to stop ongoing atrocity crimes goes hand in hand with:[102] (i) encouraging and assisting them to comply with their duties to investigate and prosecute those crimes already occurred ('positive complementarity');[103] and (ii) dividing with the ICC, particularly in cases of substantial capacity deficits, the burden of adjudicating the crimes ('cooperative complementarity').[104] As a consequence, supporting receptive states to strengthen their judicial systems and carry out national proceedings is a core component of the ICC's timely intervention.

As stated by William Burke-White[105] and Christopher Hall,[106] the Prosecutor, in order to fulfil this mandate during his preliminary examinations and investigations, may rely on those measures referred to in the previous section. In particular, the Prosecutor may train national actors in the adjudication of atrocity crimes, and may assist them in the establishment of protection programmes for victims and witnesses and effective systems of information management. He can also monitor and provide feedback regarding the development of national proceedings, and work in coordination with other ICC organs to increase the efficacy of overall preventative efforts.

It must be stressed that, despite the international cooperation of other stakeholders, the national authorities of receptive states appear to have a strong preference to receive advice and guidance directly from ICC officials. As national authorities are aware that their efforts to adjudicate atrocity crimes will be reviewed by the ICC, the ICC's advice and guidance is considered of the utmost importance to ensure the success of such efforts. As a result, the potential of the ICC to strengthen through timely intervention the rule of law and improve good governance in receptive states is major.[107] The

---

102 Both positive and cooperative complementarity appear to have been implicitly upheld, to an important extent, by the 22 June 2009 decision of the ICC Appeals Chamber in the *Katanga and Ngudjolo* case. See *Prosecutor v Mr Germain Katanga and Mathieu Ngudjolo Chui* (Decision on the Presiding Judge of the Appeals Chamber in the appeal of Germain Katanga against the Decision of Trial Chamber I of 12 June 2009 on the admissibility of the case) ICC-01/04-01/07 OA 8 (10 Jul 2009).

103 See Burke-White, 'Implementing' (Above n. 92) at 61; Hall, 'Developing' (Above n. 92) at 220. See also M.E. Cross and S. Williams, 'Recent Developments at the ICC: Prosecutor v. Germain Katanga and Mathieu Ngudjolo Chui: A Boost for Co-operative Complementarity?' (2010) 10 *Human Rights Law Review* 336, 339.

104 A. Cassese et al., 'The Rome Statute: A Tentative Assessment', in: A. Cassese et al. (eds.), *The Rome Statute of the International Criminal Court: A Commentary* (Oxford, Oxford University Press, 2002) 1906; C. Kress, '"Self-Referrals" and "Waivers of Complementarity": Some Considerations in Law and Policy' (2004) 2 *Journal of International Criminal Justice* 944, 947-8; F. Gioia, 'State Sovereignty, Jurisdiction, and "Modern" International Law: The Principle of Complementarity in the International Criminal Court' (2006) 19 *Leiden Journal of International Law* 1095, 1115.

105 Burke-White, 'Implementing' (Above n. 92) at 61.

106 Hall, 'Developing' (Above n. 92) at 220.

107 See also in this regard, W. Burke-White, 'Complementarity in Practice: The International Criminal Court as Part of a System of Multi-level Global Governance in the Democratic Republic of Congo' (2005) 18 *Leiden Journal of International Law* 557, 589-90. See also in this respect the document issued by the prosecution itself which was published just after this inaugural address was delivered. ICC Office of the Prosecutor, 'Draft Policy Paper on Preliminary Examinations' (4 Oct 2010)

preliminary examination in Colombia provides some *indicia* of this potential. Investigations of those paramilitary members demobilised in Colombia since 2003[108] did not start until May 2006, when the Constitutional Court upheld the centrepiece of the demobilisation process: the Peace and Justice Law.[109] Soon afterwards, the ICC Prosecutor made public his preliminary examination,[110] and in October 2007 and August 2008 he personally conducted two on-site visits to Colombia.[111]

Since then, the Supreme Court of Colombia has underscored the importance of focusing investigations under the Peace and Justice Law on (i) the pattern of atrocity crimes committed against the civilian population, and (ii) the structure, membership and external support of those paramilitary organisations through which the crimes were committed.[112] This has been fully reflected in the sixteen-page *Protocol for the Presentation of Evidence* issued on 23 August 2010 by the Bogotá Peace and Justice Trial Chamber.

Furthermore, since the end of 2007, the Colombian Supreme Court has also been conducting investigations and prosecutions for alleged links with paramilitary groups against a third of the members of the Colombian Parliament,[113] as well as against around twenty Governors.[114] These proceedings, which are based on confessions made by demobilised paramilitary leaders, have led so far to more than ten convictions, most of them against members of political parties that supported the Colombian Government in 2007. Such confessions have also led to the investigation in lower courts of several

---

<www.icc-cpi.int/NR/rdonlyres/9FF1EAA1-41C4-4A30-A202-174B18DA923C/282515/OTP_Draftpolicypaperonpreliminaryexaminations04101.pdf>. At the June 2010 ICC Review Conference, a proposal was made by the stocktaking bureau on the complementarity principle to task the Secretariat of the Assembly of States Parties 'facilitating the exchange of information between the Court, States Parties, signatory States, international organizations, civil society and other stakeholders, aimed at strengthening domestic jurisdictions.' (Bureau on stocktaking: Complementarity, 'Taking Stock of the Principle of Complementarity: Bridging the Impunity Gap' (18 Mar 2010) ICC-ASP/8/51, para. 54 (e)). Although this initiative may constitute an initial first step in the right direction, it is insufficient in light of the potential in strengthening rule of law and improving good governance in receptive states through timely intervention.

108 The demobilisation process is the result of the Santa Fé de Ralito Accord signed on 15 July 2003. That agreement was between the Colombian national government and the so-called *Autodefensas Unidas de Colombian* (AUC).

109 See Corte Constitucional de Colombia, sentencia C-370/ 2006 (18 May 2006). See also JE Arvelo 'International Law and Conflict Resolution in Colombia: Balancing Peace and Justice in the Paramilitary Demobilization Process' (Winter 2006) 77 *Georgetown Journal of International Law* 411.

110 See ICC Office of the Prosecutor, 'Colombia' <www.icc-cpi.int/Menus/ICC/Structure+of+the+Court/Office+of+the+Prosecutor/Comm+and+Ref/Colombia>.

111 See *ibid.*

112 See, *inter alia*, the appeal decisions of the Penal Chamber of the Colombian Supreme Court, in the cases of (i) Wilson Salazar Carrascal (a.k.a. *el loro*), Case Num. 31539 (31 Jul 2009); and (ii) Gian Carlos Gutierrez Suarez (a.k.a. *el tuerto*), Case Num. 32022 (21 Sep 2009).

113 See Verdad Abierta's information collected up to July 2010 which refers to data provided by the New Rainbow Foundation available at <www.verdadabierta.com/reconstruyendo/1856-estadisticas>.

114 *Ibid.*

hundred civil servants, local politicians and members of the armed forces and the police.[115]

It is indisputable that only a handful of high ranking military and police officers are currently facing investigation, and that the application of the Peace and Justice Law is facing significant challenges, such as (i) the lack of publicity of the criteria to select those demobilised paramilitary members investigated under such a Law; (ii) the few convictions entered so far; (iii) the extradition to the United States on drug-trafficking charges of fourteen key high-level paramilitary leaders; (iv) the lack of demobilisation of guerrilla members; and (v) the new increase in the level of violence, spurred partly by armed groups comprised of former paramilitary members.[116]

Nevertheless, in assessing whether the ongoing Colombian proceedings for atrocity crimes are contributing to strengthening the rule of law and improving good governance, one must take into consideration the long decades of mass violence in which paramilitary groups and their aides enjoyed full impunity in Colombia.

As shown by the visits of the Colombian Attorney General and an ample delegation of the Colombian Supreme Court to the ICC in 2010, the Prosecutor's preliminary examination appears to be a contributing factor to the new situation in Colombia. Nevertheless, it is difficult to measure its impact on the Colombian national authorities as there appear to be several other contributing factors, such as: (i) the conditions imposed by the US Congress to approve US military aid and favourable trade conditions for Colombia;[117] and

115 *Ibid.*

116 For a general analysis of the justice and peace process see K. Ambos, *Procedimiento de La Ley de Justicia y Paz (Ley de 2005) y Derecho Penal Internacional* (Bogotá, GTZ, Universidad de Göttingen, 2010); Comisión Colombiana de Juristas, *Anotaciones sobre la Ley de Justicia y Paz: Una Mirada desde los Derechos de las Víctimas* (Bogotá, Comisión Colombiana de Juristas, 2007). See also the recent publication by Professor Kai Ambos extended within the framework of the roundtable with non-government organisations on the situationin Colombia in The Hague organised by the Office of the ICC on 19 and 20 October 2010, K. Ambos and F. Huber, 'The Colombian Peace Process and the Principle of Complementarity of the International Criminal Court: Is there sufficient willingness and ability on the part of the Colombian authorities or should the Prosecutor open an investigation now?' (5 Jan 2011) <www.icc-cpi.int/ NR/rdonlyres/ 2770C2C8-309A-408E-A41B-0E69F098F421/282850 /civil1.pdf>.

117 The final certification by the US State Department in connection with the performance by the Colombian armed forces of the conditions relating to compliance with the conditions of respect for human rights imposed by the United States Congress took place on 9 September 2010. See in this regard, United States Embassy in Bogotá, 'Resolución y Certificación del Gobierno Colombiano y de las Fuerzas Armadas con respect a los Condicionamientos en Derechos Humanos' (15 Sep 2010) <spanish.bogota.usembassy.gov/pr_117_15092010.html>. It can also be found on the website of the Colombian Commission of Jurists report by the US State Department which analyses in detail whether or not the Colombian armed forces in 2009 complied with the requirements of respect for human rights imposed by the United States Congress. (US Department of State, 'Memorandum of Justification concerning Human Rights Conditions with respect to Assistance for the Colombian Armed Forces' (Sep 2010) <www.coljuristas.org/ LinkClick.aspx?fileticket=ksYH5X9Cvy0%3d&tabid=160&language=es-CO)>.

the judgments of the Inter-American Court of Human Rights against Colombia for paramilitary violence.[118]

In this context, further coordination between the ICC's timely intervention and those other contributing factors will increase the effectiveness in Colombia of the measures taken by the international community pursuant to the notion of responsibility to protect. In this regard, it must be noted that the need for further coordination between the United Nations and the ICC is especially acute,[119] particularly in light of their mutual recognition and commitment to cooperation,[120] as well as the existing safeguards against ICC interference with the role of the Security Council.[121]

118 See the judgments of the Inter-American Court of Human Rights in *Case of the 19 Comerciantes vs Colombia,* Series C, No 93 (5 Jul 2004); *Case of the Mapiripán Massacre vs Colombia*, Series C, no 122 (15 Sep 2005); *Case of the Pueblo Bello Massacre vs Colombia*, Series C, No 140 (31 Jan 2006); *Case of the Ituango Massacre*, Series C, No 148 (1 Jul 2006); *Case of Manuel Cepeda Vargas vs Colombia*, Series C, No 213 (26 May 2010).

119 A. Cassese, 'Is the ICC Still Having Teething Problems' (2006) 4 *Journal of International Criminal Justice* 434, 436. See also N. Jain, 'A Separate Law for Peacekeepers: The Clash between the Security Council and the International Criminal Court' (2005)16 *European Journal of International Law* 239.

120 Paragraph 7 and 9 of the Preamble of the ICC Statute reaffirms the Purposes and Principles of the UN Charter and emphasises the will of the States Parties to have the ICC established in relationship with UN system. Moreover, article 87 (7) of the Statute permits the ICC to send a finding of lack of state cooperation to the UN Security Council for its consideration. Other provisions, such as article 87 (6) of the ICC Statute, provide that the ICC may ask any intergovernmental organisation, including the United Nations, to provide information or documents, as well as other forms of cooperation agreed upon by the relevant organisation. Furthermore, article 115 of the ICC Statute establishes that the expenses of the Court and the Assembly of States Parties may be provided for by the '[f]unds provided by the United Nations, subject to the approval of the General Assembly, in particular in relation to the expenses incurred due to referrals by the Security Council. In turn, the Negotiated Relationship Agreement between the ICC and the United Nations (elaborated pursuant to article 2 of the ICC Statute) is based on mutual recognition between the UN and the ICC and a commitment to cooperation. Its preamble highlights 'the important role assigned to the International Criminal Court in dealing with the most serious crimes of concern to the international community as a whole [...] and which threaten the peace, security and well-being of the world.' On the basis of a general obligation of mutual cooperation, coordination and consultation enshrined in article 3, the Negotiated Relationship Agreement elaborates on the modalities of cooperation between both organisations in a number of areas, including UN Security Council referrals (art 17(1) of the Negotiated Relationship Agreement), UN Security Council requests for suspension of ICC investigations and prosecutions (art 17(2) of the Negotiated Relationship Agreement), UN Security Council cooperation under the condition of confidentiality (art 18(3) of the Negotiated Relationship Agreement), and UN Security Council cooperation with the ICC Prosecutor in the context of a preliminary examination (art 18(2) ICC Statute of the Negotiated Relationship Agreement).

121 Articles 12, 13, and 16 of the ICC Statute empower the UN Security Council to refer any post 1 July 2002 situation to the ICC without any jurisdictional limitation, and to request the ICC to suspend an investigation or a prosecution for renewable periods of 12 months.Moreover, the Assembly of States Parties has recently approved by consensus at the First Review Conference that the ICC will only exercise its jurisdiction over the crime of aggression after ascertaining whether the UN Security Council has made a determination of an act of aggression committed by the relevant State. In the absence of such a declaration, the ICC could only proceed if it is acting on the basis of a State Party referral or an individual communication and if the plenary of the Pre-Trial Division gives its authorisation to do so (see Assembly of States Parties, 'Amendments to the Rome Statute of the International Criminal Court on the Crime of Aggression' Annex I to Resolution RC/Res.6 (11 June 2010) art. 15 bis, para 6).

V Conclusion

The ICC's preventative mandate is an important means to fulfil the responsibility of the international community under the notion of responsibility to protect. So far, the focus has been on the ICC's efforts on general prevention by ending impunity for past atrocities. Nevertheless, the ICC's contribution to the prevention of future atrocity crimes through timely intervention is potentially even greater.

Realising this potential requires acknowledgment of the ICC's preventative role through timely intervention by the different organs of the institution. It also requires States Parties to recognise this role so as to provide the necessary resources, and extend to all atrocity crimes criminal liability for 'planning' and 'preparation'. Based on this premise, increased coordination between the ICC, the United Nations and other stakeholders will increase the preventive effect of their timely intervention.

In the end, what is at stake is whether the ICC remains as one among several mechanisms for accountability with a limited general prevention mandate; or whether, instead, it fully develops its potential to prevent atrocity crimes, strengthen the rule of law and improve good governance through timely intervention.

Acknowledgements

I would like to thank the *Rector Magnificus* and the Central Board of Utrecht University for my appointment as chair on international criminal law and international criminal procedure. Thanks are also due to the board of the Faculty of Law, Economics and Governance, and in particular the Department of Law, for the trust it has placed in me by supporting my appointment. I am committed to do my best to fulfill its expectations.

I would like to extend my gratitude and appreciation to the Willem Pompe Institute, the ICC, and the ICTY. In particular, I would like to acknowledge my gratitude to Judge Sylvia Steiner, who has been my boss and my close friend for almost a decade. She will always be unforgettable to me.

I would like to acknowledge Ambassador Juan Antonio Yañez-Barnuevo, Law Professor Maria del Carmen Calvo, William Fenrick and Pieter Kruger for having trust in me, ten years ago, when nobody else did it. My gratitude is also extended to some my colleagues here in Utrecht who have put their trust in a young Spanish professor with a "pirate accent"; John, Ige, Stijn, Francois, Dina, Chrisje, Anne-Marieke, Leo, Eric, Diana, Enrique, Jill and Dessy – thank you very much.

A mis padres Valentín y Mercedes quiero agradecerles el amor y el apoyo desinteresado que siempre me han ofrecido desde el día en que, gracias a ellos, vi la luz por primera vez. Ellos son, sin duda, los verdaderos responsables de aquello que soy hoy.

I also want to thank to my sisters Laura and Ana, who travelled yesterday from Spain to be here today. I am particularly indebted to Laura for her generosity in the most difficult of times, as well as my other siblings, Pablo, José and Elena, who unfortunately cannot be with us today. I wish them happiness and good cheer.

I would like to thank Gordon Brandt, for his invaluable help in preparing this presentation, and Sonia, Edwin, Julian, Ana Maria, Alejandro, Romina, Julieta, Teresa and Salvador who have always supported me, even in the most challenging situations. In particular, I want to extend words of encouragement and support to Sonia who is currently facing serious, but not insurmountable, health problems.

And of course I would like to also thank Paola, who has suffered through the drafting of this inaugural lecture day after day for the last year and half, and has made me believe in love again. For her, I have only two words: 'Te quiero'.

Finally, to all of you for being here on an unforgettable day; I offer my most heartfelt thanks for your presence.

And on that note, following the advice of my dear Gerda Blok and Carin Schnitger, I conclude this inaugural lecture by stating that 'Ik heb gezegd'.

De rol van het Internationaal Strafhof in het voorkomen van internationale misdrijven door middel van tijdige interventie

De rol van het Internationaal Strafhof in het voorkomen van internationale misdrijven door middel van tijdige interventie

Van de humanitaire interventie-doctrine en ex post facto tribunalen naar de notie van de verantwoordelijkheid om te beschermen en de preventieve rol van het Internationaal Strafhof

Rede uitgesproken bij de aanvaarding van
het ambt van hoogleraar Internationaal staf(proces)recht
aan de Universiteit Utrecht op 18 oktober 2010

door

Dr. Hector Olásolo

eleven
international publishing

Published, sold and distributed by Eleven International Publishing
P.O. Box 85576
2508 CG The Hague
The Netherlands
Tel.: +31 70 33 070 33
Fax: +31 70 33 070 30
e-mail: sales@budh.nl
www.elevenpub.com

Sold and distributed in USA and Canada
International Specialized Book Services
920 NE 58th Avenue, Suite 300
Portland, OR 97213-3786, USA
Tel: 1-800-944-6190 (toll-free)
Fax: +1 503 280-8832
orders@isbs.com
www.isbs.com

Eleven International Publishing is an imprint of Boom uitgevers Den Haag.

Cover photograph: ICC-CPI2006_49 031©ICC-CPI Hans Hordijk
Lay-out: Wieneke Matthijsse

ISBN 978-94-90947-40-8

Printed in The Netherlands

Mijnheer de rector magnificus,[1]

De gewelddadige geschiedenis van de twintigste eeuw heeft jammerlijk blijk gegeven van het collectieve onvermogen van internationale instituties en het ernstige falen van individuele staten om te voldoen aan hun meest basale en meest dwingende verantwoordelijkheden.[2] Vanwege de grote en langdurige kosten voor een maatschappij die te maken krijgt met ernstige internationale misdrijven ('atrocity crimes'),[3] wordt het versterken van de mogelijkheid tot preventieve actie uiterst relevant.[4] Dit komt tot uiting in de opkomende notie van de 'verantwoordelijkheid om te beschermen'.[5]

In deze rede bespreek ik de rol van het Internationaal Strafhof bij de implementatie van de notie van de 'verantwoordelijkheid om te beschermen'. Het gaat hierbij om andere instrumenten dan die welke betrekking hebben op het tegengaan van straffeloosheid van reeds gepleegde misdaden.

I Humanitaire interventie-doctrine en de verantwoordelijkheid om te beschermen

In de jaren negentig zijn verschillende internationale tribunalen met jurisdictie over reeds gepleegde internationale misdrijven opgericht door de Ver-

---

1 De auteur bedankt Gordon Brandt en Margaret Wichmann voor hun wetgeving-, jurisprudentie- en literatuuronderzoek. Ook is de auteur veel dank verschuldigd aan dr. Annemarieke Beijer, Wouter de Zanger en Wieneke Matthijsse, collega's bij het Willem Pompe Instituut, voor het vertalen en redigeren van deze tekst. Deze tekst bevat de mening van de auteur, welke niet noodzakelijkerwijs overeenkomt met die van het Internationaal strafhof, het Joegoslaviëtribunaal, de Verenigde Naties in het algemeen of de Spaanse overheid.

2 Algemene Vergadering van de Verenigde Naties (AVVN), 'Implementing the Responsibility to Protect: Report of the Secretary-General' (12 januari 2009), UN Doc A/63/677 paragrafen 5 en 6. Hierna AVVN, over Verantwoordelijkheid om te beschermen.

3 Onder de term 'atrocity crimes' versta ik hier: genocide, misdrijven tegen de menselijkheid waaronder etnische zuivering, en oorlogsmisdrijven. Zie D. Scheffer, 'Atrocity Crimes Framing the Responsibility to Protect', *Case Western Reserve Journal of International Law* 2007-2008, p. 111-136 [hierna: Scheffer, Atrocity Crimes], p. 117. Zie ook D. Scheffer, 'Genocide and Atrocity Crimes', *Genocide Studies and Prevention* 2006, 238-239. Noot van de vertaler: De oorspronkelijke tekst van Olásolo spreekt over 'atrocity crimes'. Vanwege het ontbreken van een adequate Nederlandse term is ervoor gekozen om de term 'atrocity crimes' te vertalen met 'internationale misdrijven'.

4 Zoals benadrukt in overweging 32 AVVN, over Verantwoordelijkheid om te beschermen (voetnoot 2): '[t]he difference between the two paths can amount to the choice between national potential preserved or destroyed.'

5 AVVN, over Verantwoordelijkheid om te beschermen (voetnoot 2), p. 2 en overwegingen 1-10.

enigde Naties (VN), of onder directe invloed van de Verenigde Naties.[6] Deze tribunalen worden gekenmerkt door hun primaat over nationale jurisdicties, hun tijdelijkheid en de beperking van hun jurisdictie tot een specifieke crisissituatie, zoals het uiteenvallen van het voormalig Joegoslavië of de genocide in Rwanda.[7] Zoals uitgelegd door Leila Sadat en Michael Scharf waren zij onderdeel van een grotere VN-strategie met betrekking tot situaties na afloop van het conflict en was hun primaire doel om verzoening te faciliteren.[8]

Het was niet te verdedigen dat enerzijds de basis voor juridisch ingrijpen werd uitgebreid terwijl anderzijds werd vastgehouden aan een mondiaal systeem dat internationale misdrijven tolereerde door niet in te grijpen.[9] Als gevolg hiervan werden in de jaren negentig ook de grootste ontwikkelingen in de humanitaire interventie-doctrine bewerkstelligd en werd deze doctrine toegepast in situaties als die in Somalië in 1993 en Kosovo in 1999.[10]

De humanitaire interventie-doctrine is gebaseerd op de beginselen van soevereiniteit en verantwoordelijkheid, welke kunnen worden teruggevoerd op Fransisco de Vitoria en Bartolomé de las Casas. Hun ideeën hebben in 1542 geleid tot de 'New Laws of the Indies' die, voor het eerst in de koloniale geschiedenis van Europa, de slavernij van inboorlingen afschaften.[11] In

---

6 A. Cassese, 'From Nuremberg to Rome: International Military Tribunals to the International Criminal Court', in: A. Cassese et al. (red.), *The Rome Statute to the International Criminal Court, Vol I*, Oxford: Oxford University Press, 2002, p. 10-17.

7 R. Cryer et al., *An Introduction to International Criminal Law and Procedure*, Cambridge: Cambridge University Press, 2007, p. 102-117 [hierna: Cryer, An Introduction].

8 L. Sadat, 'The Legacy of the ICTY: The International Criminal Court', *New England Law Review* 2003, p. 1073; en M. Scharf en V. Morris, *An Insider's Guide to the International Criminal Tribunal for the Former Yugoslavia, Vol I*, Irvington-on-Hudson, NY: Transnational Publishers, 1995, p. 17-36. Zie ook: Report of the Secretary-General Pursuant to Paragraph 2 of the Security Counsel Resolution 808(1993), (3 mei 1993) S/25704; Report of the Secretary-General Pursuant to Paragraph 5 of Securty Counsil resolution 955 (1994) (13 februari 1995) s/1995/134.

9 International Commission on Intervention and State Sovereignty (ICISS), '*The Responsibility to Protect'* (december 2001), <www.iciss.ca/pdf/Commission-Report.pdf> [hierna: ICISS Report]. Zie ook: Scheffer, Atrocity Crimes (voetnoot 3), p. 117.

10 Zie in het algemeen: A. Hehir, *Humanitarian Intervention: an Introduction*, Londen: Palgrave Macmillan, 2010. Voor een specifieke beschouwing over de humanitaire interventie in Kosovo: zie p. 201-220 van hetzelfde boek. Voor een specifieke beschouwing over de humanitaire interventie in Somalië, zie: F. Teson, *Humanitarian Intervention: An Inquiry into Law and Morality*, Ardsley: Transnational Publishers, 2005, p. 298 [hierna: Teson, *Humanitarian Intervention*].

11 De ideeën van Francisco de Vitoria (1483/1486-1546) en Bartolomé de las Casas (1485-1566) hebben geleid tot wetgeving inzake de goede behandeling en bescherming van de indianen. Deze wetten werden werden opgesteld om de uitbuiting van de oorspronkelijke bevolking van Amerika door grootgrondeigenaren (*Encomenderos*) tegen te gaan. Dit gebeurde door middel van een sterke beperking van de macht en heerschappij van de grondeigenaren. Franciso de Vitoria heeft zijn ideeën over legitieme soevereine macht geëxtrapoleerd naar het internationale niveau. Volgens hem dienden niet alleen in de relaties tussen individuele staten de universele rechten gerespecteerd te worden, maar was er ook een algemeen (bovenstatelijk) belang dat superieur was aan het belang van elke staat. Dientengevolge dienden relaties tussen staten niet meer beheerst te worden door machtsuitoefening, maar door recht en rechtvaardigheid. Voor de vertaling van fragmenten van Vitoria's werk *De Indis* (1532) en *De Jure belli Hispanorum in barbaros* (1532) zie zijn postume werk getiteld *Relectiones Theologicae*, bewerkt door James Brown Scott, Oceana Publications,

de vroege zeventiende eeuw onderstreepte de Jezuiet Fransisco Suarez, een vooraanstaand vertegenwoordiger van de School van Salamanca,[12] dat politieke macht voortkomt uit de consensus van de wil van vrije personen en dat het volk dus het recht heeft om machthebbers niet te gehoorzamen en zelfs om een onrechtvaardige regering omver te werpen.[13] Vervolgens ontwikkelden Hugo de Groot,[14] John Locke[15] en de achttiende-eeuwse aanhangers van de contracttheorie de notie van soevereiniteit als verantwoordelijkheid zoals we die nu kennen.

De humanitaire interventie-doctrine, die gebaseerd is op deze veronderstelling en die voor het eerst werd geformuleerd door Hersch Lauterpacht in de onmiddellijke nasleep van de Tweede Wereldoorlog,[16] rechtvaardigt een

---

1917. Ze werden opnieuw gedrukt door het Carnegie Instituut in Washington in 1964 met de bewerking van Ernesy Nys, die Vitoria's invloed op Hugo de Groot benadrukt. Zie ook B. De las Casas, *Brevísima relación de la destrucción de las Indias (A Short Account of the Destruction of the Indies)*, vertaald door Nigel Griffin, Londen: Penguin Classics, 1999. Dit is de vertaalde versie van het werk van De las Casas uit 1542. Na de goedkeuring van de 'New Laws' in 1542 werd er in de Spaanse stad Valladolid in 1550 en 1551 een debat gehouden over de behandeling van de inboorlingen van de Indiën. Twee kampen konden worden onderscheiden. Aan de ene kant beargumenteerde Bartolomé de las Casas, priester van de orde der Dominicanen en de Bisschop van Chiapas, dat de indianen vrije mensen waren in de natuurlijke orde, en dat zij, volgens de katholieke theologie, dezelfde behandeling als anderen verdienden. Aan de andere kant stelde mede-Dominicaan Juan Ginés Sepúlveda dat de indianen van nature slaven waren, en dat het in lijn met de katholieke theologie en het natuurrecht was om hen te onderwerpen aan slavernij en dienstbaarheid. De 'New Laws' werden behouden na de overwinning van De las Casas' standpunt. Zie A. Losada, *The Controversy between Sepúlveda and Las Casas in the Junta of Valladolid*, DeKalb: Northern Illinois University Press, 1971, p. 280-282. Zie ook B. Keen, *The Legacy of Bartolomé de Las Casas*, Boulder: Westview Press, 1998, p. 57-69; D.A. Brading, *The First America: the Spanish Monarchy, Creole Patriots, and the Liberal State 1492-1867*, Cambridge: Cambridge University Press, 1991, p. 80-88; A. Padgen, *The Fall of Natural Man: The American Indian and the Origins of Comparative Ethnology*, Cambridge: Cambridge University Press, 1982, p. 109; J. Crow, *The Epic of Latin America*, Berkeley: University of California Press, 1992.

12 De meest vooraanstaande leden van de School van Salamanca waren Francisco de Vitoria (1486-1546), Domingo de Soto (1494-1560), Martín de Azpilicueta (1491-1486), Tomás de Mercado (1525-1575) en Francisco Suarez (1548-1617).

13 Zie in het bijzonder F. Suárez (vertaald door G.L. Williams en H. Davis), 'Defensio Fidei Catholicae adversus Anglicanae sectae errores (The Defense of the Catholic Faith against the Errors of the Anglican)' (1613), in: F. Suarez, *Selections from three works of Francisco Suarez, S.J.: De legibus, ac deo legislatore, 1612; Defensio fidei catholicae, et apostolicae adversus anglicanae sectae errores, 1613; De triplici virtute theologica, fide, spe, et charitate, 1621*, Londen/Oxford: Clarendon Press, 1944.

14 Dit idee is terug te vinden in De Groots idee van 'dingen die publiek en eigen aan alle mensen zijn'. Zie Hugo de Groot (vertaald door R. Magoffin), *De Mare Liberum (1609)*, New York: Oxford University Press, 1916, p. 22-44; Hugo de Groot (vertaald door F. Kelsey), *Dejure Belli AC Pacis* boek II (1625), Gloucestershire: Clarendon Press, 1925, hoofdstuk 2; zie in het algemeen: H. Lauterpacht, 'The Grotian Tradition in International Law', *British Yearbook of International Law* 1946, p. 27.

15 Zie bijvoorbeeld, J. Locke 'The Second Treatise of Government' (1690), in: P. Laslet (red.), *Two Treatises of Government*, Cambridge: Cambridge University Press, 1988, p. 265.

16 H. Lauterpacht (red.), *Oppenheim's International Law: A Treatise*, Londen: Longmans Green and Company, 1947, p. 280. Zie ook P. Jessup, *A Modern Law of Nations*, New York: The Macmillan Company, 1948, p. 172-174; I. Brownlie, 'Humanitarian Intervention', in: J. Moore (red.), *Law and Civil War in the Modern World*, Baltimore: Johns Hopkins University Press, 1974, p. 217; I. Brownlie, 'The Principle of Non-Use of Force in Contemporary International Law', in:

recht op gewapende interventie in een staat die onwillig of niet in staat is om zijn eigen bevolking te beschermen tegen internationale misdrijven.[17] Volgens zijn aanhangers is een humanitaire interventie door de Verenigde Naties, of door staten met of zonder toestemming van de VN, in overeenstemming met de beginselen van soevereiniteit en territoriale integriteit, zoals omarmd door het handvest van de Verenigde Naties. Zulke beginselen, zo stellen zij, hebben als doel om de burgers van staten te beschermen, en niet de staten als entiteiten.[18] Daarom kunnen deze beginselen niet worden toegepast op staten die internationale misdrijven plegen of anderszins er niet in slagen dergelijke misdaden te voorkomen.

Toch is de humanitaire interventie-doctrine in het afgelopen decennium om verschillende redenen snel verlaten.[19] Ten eerste heeft deze gefaald om

---

W. Butler (red.), *The Non-Use of Force in International Law*, Dordrecht: Nijhoff, 1989, p. 17.

17 Volgens de aanhangers van deze doctrine is humanitaire interventie 'the proportionate transboundary help, including forcible help, provided by governments to individuals in another state who are being denied basic human rights and who themselves would be rationally willing to revolt against their oppressive government.' Zie Teson, *Humanitarian Intervention* (voetnoot 10), p. 5. Zie ook B.F. Burmester, 'On Humanitarian Intervention: The New World Order and Wars to Preserve Human Rights', *Utah Law Review* 1994, p. 269; J. Delbruck, 'A Fresh Look at Humanitarian Intervention Under the Authority of the United Nations', *Indiana Law Journal* 1992, p. 897-901; R. Gordon, 'Humanitarian Intervention by the United Nations: Iraq, Somalia, and Haiti', *Texas International Law Journal* 1996, p. 44-46; R. Lillich, 'Forcible Self Help Under International Law', *Readings in International Law from the Naval War College Review* 1980, p. 134; J. Nafziger, 'Self-Determination and Humanitarian Intervention in a Community of Power', *Denver Journal of International Law and Policy* 1991, p. 21-26. Volgens deze auteurs was humanitaire interventie niet onwettig onder artikel 2(4) van het Handvest van de Verenigde Naties, omdat (i) het niet de territoriale integriteit van een staat aantast, aangezien het doel van een dergelijke interventie er niet in is gelegen om grondgebied te verkrijgen of om bestaande grenzen te veranderen; en (ii) het niet de politieke onafhankelijkheid van staten aantast, aangezien het niet de bedoeling is om recalcitrante staten politieke dominantie van de interveniërende staat op te leggen. Bovendien was het in overeenstemming met het doel van het Handvest om mensenrechten en zelfbeschikking te bevorderen. Zie in het bijzonder R. Lillich, 'Forcible Self-Help by States to Protect Human Rights', *Iowa Law Review* 1967, p. 332-38 [hierna: Lillich, Forcible Self-Help by States]; R. Lillich, 'Humanitarian Intervention: A Reply to Ian Brownlie and a Plea for Constructive Alternatives', in: J.N. Moore (red.), *Law and Civil War in the Modern World*, Baltimore: Johns Hopkins University Press, 1974, p. 229 [hierna: Lillich, Humanitarian Intervention]; R. Lillich, 'Intervention to Protect Human Rights', *McGill Law Journal* 1969, p. 205-219 [hierna: Lillich, Intervention]; J.N. Moore, 'Toward an Applied Theory for the Regulation of Intervention', in: J.N. Moore (red.), *Law and Civil War in the Modern World*, Baltimore: Johns Hopkins University Press, 1974, p. 24-25 [hierna: Moore, Toward]; W. Reisman, 'Sovereignty and Human Rights in Contemporary International Law', *American Journal of International Law* 1990, p. 866-877 [hierna: Reisman, Sovereignty].

18 Lillich, Forcible Self-Help by States (voetnoot 17), p. 332-38; Lillich, Humanitarian Intervention (voetnoot 17), p. 229; Lillich, Intervention (voetnoot 17); Moore, 'Toward' (voetnoot 17), p. 24-25; Reisman, Sovereignty (voetnoot 17).

19 De theoretische debatten over humanitaire interventie worden samengevat in S. Murphy, *Humanitarian Intervention: The United Nations in an Evolving World Order*, Washington DC: PAIL Institute, 1996, p. 202-212; O. Ramsbotham en T. Woodhouse, *Humanitarian Intervention in Contemporary Conflict: A Reconceptualization*, Cambridge: Polity Press, 1991, p. 33-65; D. Richemond, 'Normativity in International Law: The Case of Unilateral Humanitarian Intervention', *Yale Human Rights and Development Law Journal* 2003, p. 48-49.

precieze criteria te formuleren voor de omstandigheden die aanleiding geven tot een recht tot gewapende interventie.[20]

Ten tweede werd er geen brede consensus bereikt over de geldigheid van de doctrine, aangezien door velen werd betoogd dat het VN handvest geen uitzondering kent voor het gebruik van geweld bij een humanitaire interventie.[21]

Ten derde liet de notie van humanitaire interventie, aangezien deze beperkt was tot reacties op daadwerkelijk gepleegde internationale misdrijven, de staten geen andere optie dan te kiezen tussen twee onwenselijke handelwijzen: niet ingrijpen bij een oplopend aantal burgerdoden, of militaire macht aanwenden om de bedreigde bevolking te beschermen.[22]

Als gevolg van het afnemen van de steun voor de humanitaire interventie-doctrine en de structurele beperkingen van ad hoc tribunalen, was er behoefte aan nieuwe, effectieve mechanismen om internationale misdrijven te voorkomen.

De notie van de verantwoordelijkheid om te beschermen, zoals onderschreven door de Algemene Vergadering van de VN op de Wereldtop van 2005,[23] bevestigd door de VN Veiligheidsraad in 2006,[24] en verder ontwik-

---

20 Zie in het algemeen R. Zacklin, 'Beyond Kosovo: the United Nations and Humanitarian Intervention', in: L.C. Vorah et al. (red.), *Man's Inhumanity to Man*, Den Haag: Kluwer Law International, 2003, p. 935; T. Franck, 'Legality and Legitimacy in Humanitarian Intervention', in: T. Nardin en M.S. Williams (red.), *Humanitarian Intervention*, New York: New York University Press, 2006, p. 143.

21 M. Akehurst, 'Humanitarian Intervention', in: H. Bull (red.), *World Politics*, Oxford: Clarendon Press, 1984, p. 95 en p. 104-07; en I. Brownlie, *International Law and the Use of Force by States*, Oxford: Clarendon Press, 1963, p. 338-342. Zie ook N. Ronzitti, *Rescuing Nationals Abroad Through Military Coercion and Intervention on Grounds of Humanity*, Dordrecht: Martinus Nijhoff Publishing, 1985.

22 AVVN, over Verantwoordelijkheid om te beschermen (voetnoot 2) paragrafen 5 en 6. Daar komt bij, zoals ook benadrukt door de International Commission on Intervention and State Sovereignty (ICISS): 'external military intervention for humanitarian protection purposes has been controversial both when it has happened – as in Somalia, Bosnia and Herzegovina and Kosovo – and when it has failed to happen, as in Rwanda' (ICISS Rapport (voetnoot 9), p. 7).

23 In reactie op Kofi Annans vraag tijdens het '2000 Millennium adress' heeft de Canadese regering een ICISS opgericht die onder leiding van Gareth Evans en Mohamed Sahnoun, de controversiële humanitaire interventie-doctrine heeft afgezworen om zich te richten op de nieuwe notie van de verantwoordelijkheid om te beschermen. Het rapport van het ICISS over de notie van de verantwoordelijkheid om te beschermen (zie voetnoot 9) is uitgebracht in december 2001. Voor een inzicht vanuit het perspectief van een insider in het werk van de commissie, zie: G. Evans, *The Responsibility to Protect: Ending Mass Atrocity Crimes Once and for All*, Washington D.C.: Brookings Institution Press, 2008. Zie ook A. Bellamy, *A Responsibility to Protect: the Global Effort to End Mass Atrocities*, Cambridge: Polity Press, 2009; R. Thakur, *The United Nations, Peace and Security: From Collective Security to the Responsibility to Protect*, Cambridge: Cambridge University Press, 2006, p. 245-86; T. Weiss en D. Hubert, *The Responsibility to Protect: Research, Bibliography and Background*, Ottowa: International Development Research Centre, 2001; en R. Thakur, 'Outlook: Intervention, Sovereignty and the Responsibility to Protect Experience from ICISS', *Security Dialogue* 2002, p. 323-340. De notie van de verantwoordelijkheid om te beschermen werd vervolgens onderschreven door het VN panel inzake bedreigingen, uitdagingen en verandering (zie UN Secretary-General's High-Level Panel on Threats, Challenges and Change, 'A more secure world: Our shared responsibility' (2004)) <www.un.org/secure

keld door de Secretaris-Generaal van de VN in 2009, heeft als doel deze rol te vervullen.[25]

Net als de humanitaire interventie-doctrine is de notie van de verantwoordelijkheid om te beschermen gebaseerd op de beginselen van soevereiniteit en verantwoordelijkheid. Het heeft niettemin enkele onderscheidende kenmerken die, zoals Carsten Stahn al aangaf,[26] in een korte periode brede steun hebben verworven. Ten eerste benadert de notie het dilemma van interventie eerder vanuit het perspectief van de slachtoffers van internationale misdrijven, dan vanuit het perspectief van hen die dit recht dienen te verzekeren.[27]

Ten tweede heeft deze notie niet slechts betrekking op internationale misdrijven die daadwerkelijk plaats hebben gevonden. Integendeel, de notie van verantwoordelijkheid om te beschermen vormt juist een holistische benadering van crisissituaties,[28] aangezien zij is gebaseerd op de veronderstelling dat een effectieve reactie vraagt om een interventie die start met het hanteren van preventieve maatregelen.[29] Alleen indien zulke maatregelen falen, is het nodig op internationale misdrijven te reageren.[30] Bovendien

---

world>, overwegingen 65 en 66). Op 16 september 2005 heeft de Algemene Vergadering van de VN tijdens de Wereldtop van 2005 het concept van de verantwoordelijkheid om te beschermen aangenomen (UNGA Res A/Res/60/1 (24 oktober 2005)) World Summit Outcome 2005, overwegingen 138 en 139 [hierna: UNGA Res A/Res/60/1].

24 In overweging 4 van de VN Veiligheidsraad Resolutie 1674 (2006) (28 april 2006, U.N. Doc. S/RES/1674) heeft de Veiligheidsraad de bepalingen van overwegingen 138 en 139 van de 'World Summit Outcome', 2005 aangaande de verantwoordelijkheid om bevolkingen te beschermen tegen genocide, oorlogsmisdaden, etnische zuivering en misdaden tegen de menselijkheid opnieuw bevestigd. In de tweede preambulaire overweging van Resolutie 1706 (2006) (31 augustus 2006) van de VN Veiligheidsraad over de crisis in Darfur, heeft de Veiligheidsraad haar eerdere bevestiging van die bepalingen ingetrokken.

25 AVVN, over Verantwoordelijkheid om te beschermen (voetnoot 2). Zie ook C. Joyner, 'The Responsibility to Protect: Humanitarian Concern and the Lawfulness of Armed Intervention', *Virginia Journal of International Law* 2007, p. 709.

26 C. Stahn, 'Responsibility to Protect: Political Rhetoric or Emerging Legal Norm?', *The American Journal of International Law* 2007, p. 101 en 118.

27 Idem, p. 103.

28 De behoefte aan een visie die uitgaat van meer fasen in de internationale betrokkenheid werd duidelijk tijdens de multidimensionale vredeshandhaving in de jaren 1990. Secretaris-Generaal Boutros-Ghali ontwikkelde in zijn vredesagenda een drieledige conceptie van vredeshandhaving die onderscheid maakte tussen preventieve diplomatiek, vredestichting en 'post-conflict peace building'. Zie het rapport van de Secretaris-Generaal, 'An Agenda for Peace-Preventative Diplomacy, Peacemaking, and Peace-Keeping' (1992) UN Doc. A/47/277-S/24111, p. 2, overweging 5. Sommige aspecten van dit onderscheid zijn vervolgens ontwikkeld in andere rapporten. Zie bijvoorbeeld (i) het Brahimi Rapport, dat de voortdurende ontwikkeling van preventieve actie naar vredesopbouw benadrukt (Report of the Panel on United Nations Peace Operations, UN Doc. A/55/305-S/2000/809), en (ii) het rapport 'No Exit without Strategy' uit 2001 van de Secertaris-Generaal van de VN, dat de nadruk legde op de verantwoordelijkheid na een interventie (Report of the Secretary-General, 'No Exit Without Strategy: Security Council Decision-Making and the Closure or Transition of United Nations Peacekeeping Operations' (20 april 2001) UN Doc. S/2001/394, overweging 26).

29 AVVN, over Verantwoordelijkheid om te beschermen (voetnoot 2), overwegingen 1-10.

30 Idem.

moet de keuze van het meest geschikte reactiemechanisme, waaronder ook militaire interventie, bepaald worden in het licht van de plicht langdurige vrede, een behoorlijk bestuur en rechtsstatelijke beginselen te bewerkstelligen alsmede duurzame ontwikkeling te bevorderen.[31]

Ten derde is de notie van de verantwoordelijkheid om te beschermen gebaseerd op een complementaire benadering die rust op drie pijlers. Volgens de eerste pijler is het de verantwoordelijkheid van de staten wiens bevolking in gevaar is, deze te beschermen tegen de uitlokking van en het plegen van internationale misdrijven.[32] Indien deze staten vanwege een gebrek aan capaciteit of territoriale controle daartoe niet in staat zijn, moeten andere staten en de internationale gemeenschap als geheel hen ondersteunen en bijstaan onder de tweede pijler.[33]

Indien deze maatregelen niet voldoende effect sorteren door de onwelwillendheid van het nationale gezag of een groot gebrek aan nationale capaciteit om de bevolking te beschermen, gaat de verantwoordelijkheid volgens de derde pijler over op de internationale gemeenschap om tijdige en afdoende actie te ondernemen,[34] waaronder, onder extreme omstandigheden, gewapende interventie.[35] Dit betekent dat de notie van verantwoordelijkheid om te beschermen de nadruk legt op preventie.[36] Dit heeft geleid tot een veranderde focus in het debat: van de criteria waaronder militaire inventie, met of

---

31 Idem.

32 Zie AVVN Res A/Res/60/1 (voetnoot 23), overweging 138: 'Each individual State has the responsibility to protect its populations from genocide, war crimes, ethnic cleansing and crimes against humanity. This responsibility entails the prevention of such crimes, including their incitement, through appropriate and necessary means. We [States] accept that responsibility and will act in accordance with it.' Zoals uitgelegd in AVVN, over Verantwoordelijkheid om te beschermen (voetnoot 2), overweging 18, rust de eerste pijler op oude verplichtingen in het internationaal recht, die bepalen dat de verantwoordelijkheid voor het voorkomen van mensenrechtenschendingen ligt bij het nationale beschermingssysteem van elke staat. Zie ook N. Jayawickrama, *The Judicial Application of Human Rights Law: National, Regional and International Jurisprudence*, Cambridge: Cambridge University Press, 2003, p. 46-50; B. Ramcharan, 'The National Responsibility to Protect Human Rights', *Hong Kong Law Journal* 2009, p. 369-74.

33 Zie UNGA Res A/Res/60/1 (voetnoot 23), overweging 139: (i) 'We [States] also intend to commit ourselves, as necessary and appropriate, to helping States build capacity to protect their populations from genocide, war crimes, ethnic cleansing and crimes against humanity and to assisting those which are under stress before crises and conflicts break out'; en (ii) 'The international community, through the United Nations, also has the responsibility to use appropriate diplomatic, humanitarian and other peaceful means, in accordance with Chapters VI and VIII of the Charter, to help to protect populations from genocide, war crimes, ethnic cleansing and crimes against humanity.' Bovendien verklaart overweging 140 van diezelfde verklaring: 'We [States] fully support the mission of the Special Adviser of the Secretary-General on the Prevention of Genocide.'

34 AVVN Res A/Res/60/1 (voetnoot 23), overweging 139: 'In this context, we are prepared to take collective action, in a timely and decisive manner, through the Security Council, in accordance with the Charter, including Chapter VII, on a case-by-case basis and in cooperation with relevant regional organizations as appropriate, should peaceful means be inadequate and national authorities are manifestly failing to protect their populations from genocide, war crimes, ethnic cleansing and crimes against humanity.'

35 AVVN, over Verantwoordelijkheid om te beschermen (voetnoot 2), p. 40, 50 en 56.

36 Idem, p. 1 en 2.

zonder goedkeuring van de VN, gerechtvaardigd of zelfs aangewezen is, naar de tijdige aanwending van effectieve, preventieve maatregelen.

II De twee dimensies van het preventieve mandaat van het Internationaal Strafhof: generale preventie en tijdige interventie

In de eenentwintigste eeuw is de focus van de humanitaire interventiedoctrine verschoven naar de notie van de verantwoordelijkheid om te beschermen. Tegelijkertijd heeft er ook een verschuiving plaatsgevonden van de oprichting van *ex post facto* tribunalen naar de totstandkoming en versterking van een permanent Internationaal Strafhof.

Het Internationaal Strafhof heeft, zoals onderstreept door Cherif Bassiouni,[37] een enigszins andere benadering van berechting van internationale misdrijven dan de *ex post facto* tribunalen, aangezien het: (i) door de lidstaten is opgericht door middel van een internationaal verdrag; (ii) een onafhankelijke internationale organisatie is met een permanent karakter;[38] en (iii) geen onderdeel is van een VN-strategie inzake conflictafwikkeling.[39] In het bijzonder is het Internationaal Strafhof opgericht met het doel om te handelen naar aanleiding van internationale misdrijven die zijn begaan na 1 juli 2002[40] in het grondgebied van één van de 114 lidstaten,[41] of zelfs buiten dat grondgebied indien er sprake is van een aanzienlijke betrokkenheid van één van diens staatsburgers[42] of er een verwijzing door de VN Veiligheidsraad heeft plaatsgevonden.[43] Voorts is het Internationaal Strafhof werkzaam op basis van het complementariteitsbeginsel welke bepaalt dat het slechts jurisdictie kan uitoefenen indien staten inactief zijn, of indien staten niet bereid of niet bij machte zijn om daadwerkelijk een vervolging uit te voeren.[44]

---

37 M.C. Bassiouni 'The Making of the International Criminal Court', in: M.C. Bassiouni (red.), *International Criminal Law Vol 3,* Leiden: Martinus Nijhoff Publishers, 2008, p. 117-153.

38 'Rome Statute of the International Criminal Court', UN Diplomatic Conference of Plenipotentiaries on the Establishment of an International Criminal Court (Rome 15 juni-17 juli 1998) (17 juli 1998) UN Doc A/Conf. 183/9 [hierna: Statuut van Rome], artikelen 1 en 4.

39 Het Internationaal Strafhof heeft zijn eigen politieke en financiële organen, waaronder een Vergadering van Staten die Partij zijn, een Secretariaat van de Vergadering en een Budget en Financiën Commissie (zie artikel 112 van het Statuut van Rome en de *ICC Financial Regulations and Rules*). Bovendien bezit het, zoals blijkt uit artikel 4 van het Statuut van Rome, internationale rechtspersoonlijkheid en de handelingsbevoegdheid die nodig is voor de uitoefening van zijn taken en de verwezenlijking van zijn doelstellingen.

40 Zie artikel 11 van het Statuut van Rome.

41 Zie artikel 12 van het Statuut van Rome.

42 Zie artikel 12 van het Statuut van Rome.

43 Zie artikelen 12 en 13 (b) van het Statuut van Rome.

44 Zie overweging 10 van de preambule van het Statuut van Rome en artikelen 1 en 17 van het Statuut van Rome. Zie ook *Situation in the Democratic Republic of the Congo* (Judgment on the Appeal of Mr. Germain Katanga Against the Oral Decision of Trial Chamber II of 12 June 2009 on the Admissibility of the Case) ICC-01/04-01/070A8 (25 september 2009).

Er is een duidelijk verband tussen de notie van de verantwoordelijkheid om te beschermen en het mandaat van het Internationaal Strafhof, aangezien beide zich richten op toekomstige 'situaties' waarin internationale misdrijven worden gepleegd.[45] Bovendien gaan beide uit van de primaire verantwoordelijkheid van de betrokken staten. Afgelopen jaar heeft Ban Ki-moon, Secretaris-Generaal van de VN, verwezen naar het Statuut van het Internationaal Strafhof als één van de voornaamste instrumenten in verband met de verantwoordelijkheid om te beschermen.[46]

In dit opzicht moet worden opgemerkt dat zowel het Internationaal Strafhof als *ex post facto* juridische instituties een verplichting hebben tot het beëindiging van straffeloosheid. Dit ter bevordering van: (i) positieve generale preventie, door handhaving van internationaal strafrecht en het versterken van de maatschappelijke kernwaarden die daarin beschermd worden; en (ii) negatieve generale preventie of afschrikking als gevolg van het uitdragen van de boodschap aan de wereldleiders dat zij die betrokken zijn bij internationale misdrijven daar niet mee weg zullen komen.[47] Een dergelijk 'commitment' wordt vervuld door een combinatie van juridisch optreden, betrekkingen met een aantal externe relaties, 'outreach' en publieke voorlichting.[48] De inspanningen van het Internationaal Strafhof ter generale preventie kunnen VN-functionarissen en andere belanghebbenden helpen bij het onder de aandacht brengen (onder de tweede en derde pijler van de verantwoordelijkheid om te beschermen) van zowel de kosten van betrokkenheid bij internationale misdrijven als de voordelen van het stoppen daarmee.[49]

Niettemin heeft het preventieve mandaat van het Internationaal Strafhof, in tegenstelling tot dat van de *ex post facto* juridische instituties, een tweede dimensie. Die dimensie bestaat uit de tijdige interventie in situaties waarin er sprake is van een concrete dreiging dat internationale misdrijven zullen gaan plaatsvinden, of waarin internationale misdrijven al plaatsvinden. Het preventieve mandaat wordt vooral vervuld door de aanklager van het Internationaal Strafhof door middel van zijn voorbereidende onderzoeken ('preliminary examinations and investigations'), en kan een breed scala aan situa-

---

45 De notie van de verantwoordelijkheid om te beschermen heeft betrekking op vier specifieke misdrijven (genocide, misdrijven tegen de menselijkheid, oorlogsmisdrijven en etnische zuivering), die, samen met het misdrijf agressie, ook de jurisdictie *ratione materiae* van het Internationaal Strafhof teweegbrengen (artikel 5 van het Statuut van Rome). Toch is het belangrijk om te benadrukken dat de ICISS een bredere toepasbaarheid van de notie van de verantwoordelijkheid om te beschermen voor ogen had (zie ICISS Report (voetnoot 9)). Over de discussie aangaande de mogelijkheid van een bredere toepasbaarheid van de notie van de verantwoordelijkheid om te beschermen, zie Scheffer, *Atrocity Crimes* (voetnoot 3), p. 113-116.

46 AVVN, over Verantwoordelijkheid om te beschermen (voetnoot 2), overweging 19.

47 Cryer, *An Introduction* (voetnoot 7), p. 22-39.

48 Internationaal Strafhof, 'Outreach', <www.icc-cpi.int/Menus/ICC/Structure+of+the+Court/> (laatstelijk geraadpleegd op 20 december 2010).

49 AVVN, over Verantwoordelijkheid om te beschermen (voetnoot 2), overwegingen 19 en 53.

ties omvatten. Dit komt tot uitdrukking in: (i) de 9000 'communications' die de aanklager tot op heden van individuen in meer dan 140 landen heeft ontvangen;[50] en (ii) de diversiteit van geografische locaties waar 'preliminary examinations or investigations' zijn gestart sinds 2003. Deze hebben plaatsgevonden in onder andere: Afghanistan, de Centraal-Afrikaanse Republiek, Colombia, Darfur, De Democratische Republiek Congo, Georgië, Guinee, Irak, Ivoorkust, Kenia, Palestina, Uganda en Venezuela.[51]

Aangezien de notie van de verantwoordelijkheid om te beschermen de nadruk legt op preventie door middel van tijdige interventie, kan de tijdige interventie door het Internationaal Strafhof een unieke bijdrage leveren aan het vervullen van de verantwoordelijkheid van de internationale gemeenschap onder de tweede en derde pijler van die notie.

III De tijdige interventie door het Internationaal Strafhof als gevolg van een reële dreiging dat internationale misdrijven zullen worden begaan

Internationale misdrijven zijn niet onvermijdbaar. Het duurt lang om ze te plannen en voor te bereiden, aangezien zij een collectieve inspanning en een organisatorische context vereisen.[52] Bovendien is er meestal voldoende informatie over dreigende internationale misdrijven die, hoe betreurenswaardig ook, vaak wordt genegeerd of gebagatelliseerd door vooraanstaande nationale en internationale machthebbers met concurrerende politieke agenda's.[53] Aldus zijn wettelijke bepalingen over het plannen, voorbereiden en het uitlokken van en de poging tot het plegen van internationale misdrijven van groot belang voor de effectiviteit van preventieve inspanningen door middel van tijdige interventie.

Het kan dus geen verrassing zijn dat – behalve voor de definitie van genocide, die letterlijk is overgenomen uit het Genocideverdrag van 1948[54] –

---

50 Tot op heden heeft de Aanklager 8733 individuele 'communications' ontvangen. Zie Internationaal Strafhof, 'Communications, Referrals, and Preliminary Examinations', <www.icc-cpi.int/ Menus/ ICC/Structure+of+the+Court/Office+of+the+Prosecutor/Comm+and+Ref/ Communications+and+ Referrals.htm> (laatstelijk geraadpleegd op 20 december 2010).

51 Idem.

52 K. Ambos, 'Epilogue: Future Developments of International Criminal Law in relation to the Responsibility of Superiors for International Crimes', in: H. Olásolo, *The Criminal Responsibility of Senior Political and Military Leaders as Principals to International Crimes*, Londen: Hart Publishers, 2009, p. 333.

53 AVVN, over Verantwoordelijkheid om te beschermen (voetnoot 2), overweging 6.

54 Genocide is de enige uitzondering aangezien de definitie daarvan, inclusief de verwijzingen naar samenspanning, uitlokking en poging, letterlijk is overgenomen door de statuten van *ex post facto* instituten zoals het ICTY, het ICTR en het Speciale Hof voor Sierra Leone, uit de tekst van het Verdrag inzake de Voorkoming en de Bestraffing van Genocide uit 1948. In dit verdrag worden in artikel 3 de samenspanning om genocide te plegen, het rechtstreeks en openbaar aanzetten tot genocide en de poging tot het plegen van genocide expliciet strafbaar gesteld. Zie ook J. Ohlin,

het uitgangspunt dat het Statuut van het Internationaal Strafhof hanteert behoorlijk anders is dan dat van de statuten van de *ex post facto* tribunalen. Zoals William Schabas stelt, zouden in het uitgangspunt van de statuten van laatstgenoemde instituties bepalingen over plannen, voorbereiden, aanzetten en poging simpelweg overbodig zijn geweest en dergelijke bepalingen zijn daarin dan ook niet opgenomen.[55]

Artikel 25 van het Statuut van het Internationaal Strafhof voorziet in aansprakelijkheid voor poging in relatie tot alle internationale misdrijven, niet alleen tot genocide, en verbindt dergelijke aansprakelijkheid aan het nemen van stappen waardoor de uitvoering van het misdrijf wezenlijk in gang wordt gezet.[56] Hoewel deze definitie meer vereist dan slechts het maken van plannen, rijst de vraag waar de grens moet worden getrokken tussen louter voorbereidingshandelingen en gedragingen die te beschouwen zijn als een wezenlijke stap in de uitvoering van internationale misdrijven.[57] Noch het Statuut van het Internationaal Strafhof noch de jurisprudentie van de overige internationale tribunalen geeft duidelijkheid hierover.[58]

Sommige nationale stelsels, zoals dat van Duitsland, hebben een striktere benadering gekozen, en vereisen een directe beweging richting het plegen van het misdrijf.[59] Andere stelsels, zoals dat van de Verenigde Staten, hanteren een bredere opvatting door het bezit van goederen bestemd tot het plegen van het misdrijf en het opsporen van de beoogde slachtoffers van de misdaad, strafbaar te stellen.[60]

Zou de jurisprudentie van het Internationaal Strafhof daarom een minder strikte benadering moeten omarmen? Aansprakelijkheid voor een poging kan situaties omvatten zoals die zich in Rwanda hebben voorgedaan, waar vanaf januari 1993 zestien maanden achter elkaar meer dan een half miljoen machetes werden geïmporteerd en verspreid, evenals vuurwapens en granaten, onder het mom van een zelfverdedigingsprogramma.[61]

'Attempt to Commit Genocide', in: P. Gaeta (red.), *The UN Genocide Convention: A Commentary*, Oxford: Oxford University Press, 2009, hoofdstuk 9, p. 173-185, m.n. p. 183 [hierna Ohlin, Attempt]; A. Eser, 'Individual Criminal Responsibility', in: A. Cassese, P. Gaeta en J.R.W.D. Jones (red.), *Rome Statute of the International Criminal Court: A Commentary Vol I*, Oxford: Oxford University Press, 2002 [hierna Eser, Individual], p. 807 e.v.; K. Ambos, 'Article 25 Individual Criminal Responsibility', in: O. Triffterer (red.), *Commentary on the Rome Statute of the International Criminal Court,* Oxford/München: Hart Publishing and Verlag C.H. Beck, 2008, p. 764 e.v. [hierna: Ambos, Individiual Criminal Responsibility].

55 W.A. Schabas, *Genocide in International Law*, Cambridge: Cambridge University Press, 2000, p. 281 [hierna: Schabas, Genocide].

56 Zie artikel 25 (3) (f) van het Statuut van Rome.

57 Ohlin, Attempt (voetnoot 54), p. 178.

58 Idem, p. 178 en 182-184.

59 Zie StGB § 22. Zie ook Eser, Individual (voetnoot 54), p. 812.

60 Zie ook United States Model Penal Code, § 5.01(1)(c). Zie ook G.P. Fletcher, *Rethinking Criminal Law*, New York: Oxford University Press, 2000, p. 180.

61 Prosecutor v. Nahimana et al., (Judgment) ICTR-99-52-T (3 december 2003) overweging 113.

Artikel 25 van het Statuut van het Internationaal Strafhof verbindt ook strafrechtelijke aansprakelijkheid aan het rechtstreeks en openlijk anderen aanzetten tot het plegen van genocide.[62] Ondanks de beperking tot het misdrijf genocide, kan het bereik van dit artikel aanzienlijk zijn in situaties zoals die in Rwanda, waar de media vanaf 1991 Hutu's systematisch hebben aangespoord tot geweld tegen Tutsi's,[63] of die in Cambodja, waar de radio van de Rode Khmer jaren achter elkaar luisteraars heeft aangespoord de bevolking van Cambodja te 'zuiveren'.[64]

Het misdrijf van agressie of 'crime of agression' (waarvan de definitie is vastgesteld op de eerste herzieningsconferentie van het Internationaal Strafhof in juni 2010) verbindt strafrechtelijke aansprakelijkheid aan het 'plannen' en 'voorbereiden' van een daad van agressie.[65] Dit brengt het Statuut van het Internationaal Strafhof meer in overeenstemming met de meeste nationale stelsels, waarin strafrechtelijke aansprakelijkheid zich kan voordoen als gevolg van een afspraak om een misdrijf te begaan, deelneming aan het opstellen van een crimineel plan, of het bijdragen aan het tot stand brengen van de voorwaarden voor het uitvoeren van een dergelijk plan.[66] Als

---

62 Ongeacht of de genocide daadwerkelijk plaats heeft gevonden. Zie hierover *Prosecutor v. Akayesu* (Judgment) ICTR-96-4-T TC 2 (2 september 1998) overweging 561. Zie ook J. Ohlin, 'Incitement and Conspiracy to Commit Genocide', in: P. Gaeta (red.), *The UN Genocide Convention: A Commentary*, Oxford: Oxford University Press, 2009, hoofdstuk 10, p. 186-204, m.n. p. 192-195. Zie in het bijzonder artikel 25 (3)(e) van het Statuut van Rome. Op dit specifieke punt is het Statuut van het Internationaal Strafhof iets beperkter dan zowel het Genocideverdrag als de statuten van de andere internationale en geïnternationaliseerde hoven die, hoewel beperkt tot genocide, de notie van 'samenspanning' hebben opgenomen.

63 *Prosecutor v. Nahimana et al.* (Appeal Judgment) ICTR-99-52-A (28 november 2007), overwegingen 41 and 45. Zie ook J.P. Chrétien, *Rwanda: Les Medias du Génocide*, Karthala: Reporters sans Frontiers, 2002. In het bijzonder is er, ondanks verschillende rapporten opgesteld tijdens die kritieke maanden door de *United nations Assistance Mission* in Rwanda en de *Special Rapporteur on extrajudicial, arbitrary or summary executions* over de opruiende programmering van het radiostation *des Milles Collines*, geen poging ondernomen door de internationale gemeenschap om zulke uitzendingen te verhinderen. Zie Secretaris-Generaal van de Verenigde Naties, 'Report of the Secretary-General on the Situation in Rwanda' (31 mei 1994) S/1994/640, overweging 11; Secretaris-Generaal van de Verenigde Naties, 'Letter Dated 15 December 1999 From the Secretary-General addressed to the President of the Security Council' (16 december 1999) S/1999/1257, bijlage, I; Mensenrechtencommissie van de Verenigde Naties, 'Report of the Special Rapporteur on Extrajudicial, Arbitrary or Summary Executions, Mr B.W. Ndiaye, on his Mission to Rwanda from 8 to 17 April 1993' (11 augustus 1993) E/CN.4/1994/7/Add.1.

64 BBC, *Summary of World Broadcasts*, FE/5813/A3/2, 15 mei 1978.

65 Zie bijlage I bij Resolution RC/Res.6 (11 juni 2010) getiteld 'Amendments to the Rome Statute of the International Criminal Court on the Crime of Agression', artikel 8 bis, lid 1.

66 De reikwijdte van het nationale strafrecht dat dit soort gedragingen strafbaar stelt (ongeacht de vraag of het misdrijf vervolgens is voltrokken of is aangevangen) is, in belangrijke mate, gebruikt om die situaties aan te pakken waarin meer personen gezamenlijk crimineel handelen om economische doelen (zoals bij mensenhandel, drugshandel, wapenhandel en witwassen) of politieke doelen (zoals bij terrorisme) na te streven. Het kan dan ook niet als een verrassing komen dat nationale jurisdicties hun strafbaarstelling van voorbereidingshandelingen hebben uitgebreid met voorbereiding van internationale misdrijven, die immers, behalve dat ze de meest diepgaande inbreuken op de kern van de maatschappelijke waarden van de internationale gemeenschap vormen, ook een 'unieke omvang' hebben, van 'collectieve aard' zijn en plaatsvinden in een 'organisatorische context'.

het tegenwoordig op nationaal niveau breed geaccepteerd is dat strafrechtelijke aansprakelijkheid zich voordoet bij zulke voorbereidende handelingen, dan is er inderdaad geen rechtvaardiging om anders te oordelen op het internationale niveau in relatie tot vergrijpen die zo ernstig zijn als internationale misdrijven.[67]

Hoewel de bestaande bepalingen over poging en uitlokking een voldoende basis vormen voor tijdige interventie van het Internationaal Strafhof, zal het uitbreiden van de aansprakelijkheid voor het plannen en voorbereiden van alle internationale misdrijven de preventieve rol van het Internationaal Strafhof significant versterken.[68] Bovendien zal door te concentreren op deze vroege fase van het *iter criminis* de controverse over sommige vormen van strafrechtelijke aansprakelijkheid (zoals onderstreept door Kai Ambos,[69] George Fletcher,[70] Göran Sluiter,[71] Herman van der Wilt,[72] Elies van Slie-

---

67 Zie de verschillende benaderingen die Cassese en Fletcher hanteren bij dit onderwerp in relatie tot de samenspanning om genocide te plegen: A. Cassese, 'Jurisdiction *ratione materiae* – Genocide', in: A. Cassese, P. Gaeta en J.R.W.D. Jones (red.), *The Rome Statute of the International Criminal Court: A Commentary*, Oxford: Oxford University Press, 2002, p. 347; G.P. Fletcher, 'Amicus Curiae Brief of Specialists in Conspiracy and International Law in Support of Petitioner', *WestLaw* 2006, 53979, ingediend in *Hamdan v. Rumsfeld*, 548 U.S. 557 (2006), 12. Bovendien was, volgens Schabas, het niet opnemen van samenspanning tot het plegen van genocide in het Statuut van Rome een gevolg van de onoplettendheid van uitgeputte opstellers. Zie Schabas, Genocide (voetnoot 55), p. 264.

68 Vooral de uitsluiting van de notie van samenspanning van artikel 25(3) van het Statuut van Rome (ook in relatie tot het misdrijf van genocide) lijkt ongerechtvaardigd, in het bijzonder gezien de brede acceptatie van deze notie met betrekking tot minder ernstige misdrijven in de nationale wettelijke systemen. De ratio van de strafbaarstelling van samenspanning is dat door het opstellen van een gezamenlijk plan door twee of meer personen om een serieus misdrijf te begaan, het risico op een inbreuk op het maatschappelijk belang dat wordt aangetast indien het betreffende misdrijf wordt voltooid, ernstig wordt vergroot. Dit risico wordt verder vergroot indien de bedenkers van het plan om het misdrijf te plegen de eerste stappen zetten ter voorbereiding van de daadwerkelijke uitvoering van het criminele plan. Logischerwijs wordt het risico hoger naarmate de hiërarchische positie van de betrokkenen bij het plannen van het misdrijf hoger is. Het is evenzeer logisch dat hoe zwaarder de inbreuk op een kernwaarde van de maatschappij is, hoe gerechtvaardigder een vroege ingreep in eerste fase van de *iter criminis* om de uitvoering van een misdrijf te voorkomen, is. De notie van samenspanning lijkt dientengevolge vooral geschikt om de daadwerkelijke uitvoering van (de meest serieuze) internationale misdrijven door hoge politieke en militaire leiders te voorkomen. Het niet opnemen van deze notie in de jurisdictie van het Internationaal Strafhof lijkt ongerechtvaardigd, gezien deze omstandigheden en het feit dat het misdrijf wel is opgenomen in het Genocideverdrag, in de verdragen van de *ad hoc* tribunalen en in nationale jurisdicties. Dit is temeer zo als we in ogenschouw nemen dat het misdrijf van agressie, zoals in juni 2010 goedgekeurd op de eerste herzieningsconferentie van het Internationaal Strafhof, ook voorbereidende handelingen die lijken op samenspanning (zoals het maken van plannen) in zich bergt.

69 K. Ambos, 'Joint Criminal Enterprise and Command Responsibility', *Journal of International Criminal Justice* 2007, p. 167-176.

70 G. Fletcher en J. Ohlin, 'Reclaiming Fundamental Principles of Criminal Law in the Darfur Case', *Journal of International Criminal Justice* 2005, p. 539-561.

71 A. Zahar en G. Sluiter, *International Criminal Law: A Critical Introduction*, Oxford: Oxford University Press, 2007, p. 221-257.

72 H. van der Wilt, 'Joint Criminal Enterprise Possibilities and Limitations', *Journal of International Criminal Justice* 2007, p. 91-108.

dregt,[73] Thomas Weigend,[74] en Gerard Werle[75]) verminderen, aangezien hoge leiders meestal direct betrokken zijn bij het plannen en voorbereiden van internationale misdrijven.[76] Dit zou ook in overeenstemming zijn met de door het Internationaal Strafhof gehanteerde eis dat het om zeer ernstige misdrijven moet gaan (de 'gravity threshold') en Luis Moreno-Ocampo's beleid dat het hof zich moet het concentreren op de meest verantwoordelijke personen.[77]

Zodra een individuele communicatie[78] of een verwijsbrief ('letter of referal')[79] wezenlijke aanwijzingen van een poging of uitlokking bevat, zal de aanklager van het Internationaal Strafhof een voorlopig onderzoek moeten starten.[80] Dit onderzoek heeft als doel om te kunnen onderscheiden tussen: (i) situaties die een officieel onderzoek verlangen; en (ii) situaties die beter met andere middelen kunnen worden afgehandeld.[81]

Voor een dergelijke beslissing volstaat het niet om informatie over de beschuldigingen van poging of uitlokking te verzamelen en te analyseren. Het is noodzakelijk om de beschikbare informatie te beoordelen en te kijken naar onder andere: (i) de ontvankelijkheid van de relevante 'situatie' als gevolg van mogelijk niet-handelen, onwelwillendheid of onvermogen van nationale autoriteiten en de ernst van het geweld, en (ii) mogelijke inhoudelijke redenen om aan te nemen dat het onderzoek niet in het belang van een goede rechtsbedeling zou zijn.[82]

---

73 E. van Sliedregt, 'Joint Criminal Enterprise as a Pathway to Convicting Individuals for Genocide', *Journal of International Criminal Justice* 2007, p. 184-207.

74 T. Weigend, 'Intent, Mistake of Law and Co-Perpetration in the *Lubanga* Decision on Confirmation of Charges', *Journal of International Criminal Justice* 2008, p. 471-487.

75 G. Werle, 'Individual Criminal Responsibility in Article 25 ICC Statute', *Journal of International Criminal Justice* 2007, p. 953-975.

76 Deze situatie gaat doorgaans gepaard met de bewuste instemming van een andere sector van het leiderschap, die zich onthoudt van actieve betrokkenheid, maar die niet de maatregelen neemt die in haar macht liggen om de plannen en/of voorbereidingen te stoppen.

77 Zie *ICC Office of the Prosecutor*, 'Paper on Some Policy Issues before the Office of the Prosecutor' (september 2003).

78 Zie artikelen 13 (c) en 15 (1) van het Statuut van Rome.

79 Zie artikelen 13 (a) en (b), 14 en 53 (1) van het Statuut van Rome.

80 Alle natuurlijke personen en rechtspersonen hebben niet alleen het recht tot toegang tot het Internationaal Strafhof door middel van individuele communicaties en, als het gaat om staten die partij zijn bij het Statuut of de Veiligheidsraad, verwijsbrieven, maar ook het recht om geïnformeerd te worden over de redenen waarom de Aanklager van het Internationaal Strafhof een onderzoek niet wil voortzetten. Zie artikelen 15 (6) en 53 (3) van het Statuut van Rome en Regels 104 en 105 van de *Rules of Procedure and Evidence*. Zie ook H. Olásolo, *The Triggering Procedure of the International Criminal Court*, Den Haag: Martinus Nijhoff Publishers, 2005, p. 65-70 [hierna: Olásolo, Triggering Procedure].

81 Olásolo, Triggering Procedure (voetnoot 80), p. 39-47. Zie ook Internationaal Strafhof, Regulations of the Office of the Prosecutor (23 april 2009) ICC-BD/05-01-09, artikelen 25-29.

82 Volgens de artikelen 15 (3) en (4) en 53 (1) van het Statuut van Rome, en Regel 48 van de *Rules of Procedure and Evidence* zijn dit de verschillende elementen van het criterium '*redelijke basis* om tot een onderzoek over te gaan', waaraan voldaan moet zijn wil het Internationaal Strafhof een officieel onderzoek naar een situatie kunnen doen. Dit is benadrukt door de *Pre-Trial Chamber* in de recente beslissing in de situatie aangaande Kenia (Decision Pursuant to Article 15 of the Rome

Dientengevolge kan de aanklager, zoals Antonio Cassese[83] en David Scheffer[84] duidelijk hebben gemaakt, op gepaste wijze reageren op basis van de (niet) ontvankelijkheidsgronden of gronden aangaande een goede rechtsbedeling indien nationale autoriteiten belangrijke stappen ondernemen om internationale misdrijven daadwerkelijk te voorkomen. Bovendien zullen, ingevolge artikel 25 van het Statuut van het Internationaal Strafhof, zij die een begin hebben gemaakt met de uitvoering van internationale misdrijven door middel van een wezenlijke stap niet aansprakelijk zijn indien zij hun inspanningen om de misdrijven te plegen staken, of anderszins de uitvoering van die misdrijven voorkomen.[85] Aldus kan de aanklager zijn voorlopige onderzoek naar aanleiding van beschuldigingen van poging of uitlokking sluiten indien deze tijdige interventie heeft bijgedragen aan het succesvol onschadelijk maken van de dreiging van internationale misdrijven.

Hoewel de aanklager in deze fase geen dwangmaatregelen kan inzetten[86] en in deze fase niet alle vormen van samenwerking met de lidstaten mogelijk zijn,[87] moet het potentieel van voorlopig onderzoek om nationale autoriteiten aan te sporen niet onderschat worden. Zoals verschillende voorlopige onderzoeken, onder andere in Georgië,[88] Guinee[89] en Palestina,[90] hebben laten

---

Statute on the Authorization of an Investigation into the Situation in the Republic of Kenya) ICC-01/09 (31 maart 2010), overwegingen 26-35.

83 A. Cassese, *International Criminal Law*, Oxford: Oxford University Press, 2008, p. 395-409.

84 D. Scheffer en A. Cox, 'The Constitutionality of the Rome Statute of the International Criminal Court', *Journal of Criminal Law and Criminology* 2008, p. 983-1068.

85 Artikel 25 (3)(f) van het Statuut van Rome verkaart: '[indien die persoon] een poging doet een dergelijk misdrijf te begaan door stappen te nemen waardoor de uitvoering van het misdrijf wezenlijk in gang wordt gezet, maar het misdrijf niet wordt voltrokken ten gevolge van omstandigheden die onafhankelijk zijn van de bedoelingen van de persoon. Een persoon die echter de poging tot het begaan van het misdrijf staakt of anderszins de voltrekking van het misdrijf verhindert, is niet strafbaar krachtens dit Statuut ter zake van de poging tot het begaan van dat misdrijf, indien die persoon volledig en vrijwillig van het misdadig doel heeft afgezien.' Zie Ambos, Individual Criminal Responsibility (voetnoot 54), p. 764. Zie ook Ohlin, Attempt (voetnoot 54), p. 175-177.

86 Bij de aanvang van het onderzoek kan de Aanklager ook gebruik maken van maatregelen van dwingende aard en een beroep doen op de assistendie door de staten voor wat betreft de handelingen genoemd in artikel 93 van het Statuut van het Internationaal Strafhof. Zie artikelen 54, 57 en 93 van het Statuut van Rome. Het 'vermommen' van een artikel 54-onderzoek als een artikel 15(2)-onderzoek zou in strijd zijn met de beperkte reikwijdte van het laatstgenoemde artikel. Zie Olasolo, Triggering Procedure (voetnoot 80), p. 59. Zie, voor een andere mening: M. Bergsmo, J. Pejic, 'Article 15', in: O. Triffterer (red.), *Commentary on the Rome Statute of the International Criminal Court*, Oxford/München: Hart Publishing and Verlag C.H. Beck, 2008, p. 366.

87 De vormen van assistentie die in artikel 93 van het Statuut van Rome worden genoemd en waar de Aanklager in deze fase gebruik van kan maken zijn: (i) de identificatie en lokalisering van personen of goederen; (ii) het vrijwillige verhoor van slachtoffers en getuigen in het grondgebied van de lidstaten; (iii) de betekening van documenten, met inbegrip van gerechtelijke documenten; (iv) het verstrekken van verslagen en documenten, met inbegrip van officiële akten en documenten; (v) het onderzoek van locaties; en (vi) elke andere vorm van rechtshulp van niet-dwingende aard die niet is verboden bij de wet van de aangezochte Staat. Zie Olasolo, Triggering Procedure (voetnoot 80), p. 60.

88 Met betrekking tot het voorlopige onderzoek naar de situatie in Georgië heeft, de Georgische minister van Justitie de Aankager bezocht in Den Haag nadat deze zijn voorlopige onderzoek op 14 augustus 2008 bekend heeft gemaakt. Rusland, geen partij bij het Statuut, heeft de Aanklager 3.817 communi-

zien, kan de aanklager, naast het ontvangen van getuigenverklaringen en het zoeken van informatie bij betrouwbare bronnen:[91] (i) missies naar de relevante staten sturen; (ii) nationale delegaties van regeringen, vertegenwoordigers van gerechtshoven, oppositieleiders en NGO's ontvangen in Den Haag; (iii) advies geven over de maatregelen die op nationaal niveau genomen moeten worden om de dreiging van internationale misdrijven onschadelijk te maken; (iv) met de VN en andere belanghebbenden overleggen over een preventiestrategie; (v) informatie uitwisselen met nationale en internationale actoren; en (vi) in de media de ontwikkeling van de gebeurtenissen en de mate van medewerking van de nationale autoriteiten uiteenzetten.[92]

Het gebruik van diplomatieke en mediakanalen om de wereld te wijzen op de plannen van hoge leiders om internationale misdrijven te plegen kan, samen met het benadrukken van de mogelijkheid om vervolging voor het Internationaal Strafhof te voorkomen indien zij hun plannen staken en de nodige preventieve maatregelen nemen, een krachtig wapen zijn.

Bovendien biedt het Statuut van het Internationaal Strafhof vanuit het perspectief van het tijdig reageren op een wezenlijke dreiging van internationale misdrijven, ongekende mogelijkheden. Waar andere organen van de internationale gemeenschap zoals de VN-veiligheidsraad of de Algemene Vergadering van de VN meestal lange onderhandelingen nodig hebben voordat ze kunnen beslissen om in te grijpen, hoeft de Aanklager van het Internationaal Strafhof geen belanghebbenden te consulteren voordat hij een voorlopig onderzoek kan openen.

---

caties gestuurd. De Aanklager heeft informatie gevraagd aan de regeringen van Rusland en Georgië op 27 augustus 2008, beiden hebben daarop geantwoord. Twee onderzoeken ter plaatse zijn uitgevoerd in Georgië in november 2008 en juni 2010, en één in Rusland in maart 2010. Zie Internationaal Strafhof, 'Georgia', <www.icc-cpi.int/Menus/ICC/Structure+of+the+Court/Office+of+the+Prosecutor/Comm+And+Ref/Georgia/> (laatstelijk geraadpleegd op 20 december 2010).

89 Met betrekking tot het voorlopige onderzoek naar de situatie in Guinee heeft, sinds de Aanklager zijn voorlopige onderzoek op 14 oktober 2009 bekend heeft gemaakt, overleg plaatsgevonden met president Campaore van Burkina Faso (mediator voor de contactgroep over Guinee) en president Wade van Senegal, om ervoor te zorgen dat zij op de hoogte zijn van het werk van de Aanklager; in februari en maart 2010 hebben ontmoetingen in Guinee plaatsgevonden onder andere met de minister van Justitie van Guinee, kolonel Lohalamou. Ontmoetingen met Guinese rechters hebben plaatsgevonden op 19-21 mei 2010. Zie Internationaal Strafhof, 'Guinea', <www.icc-cpi.int/Menus/ICC/Structure+of+the+Court/Office+of+the+Prosecutor/Comm+>.

90 Met betrekking tot het voorlopige onderzoek naar de Palestijnse situatie hebben een delegatie van de Palestijnse Nationale Autoriteit en vertegenwoordigers van de Arabischa Liga de Aanklager bezocht op 15 en 16 oktober 2009 en op 11 januari 2010. Zie Internationaal Strafhof, 'Palestine', beschikbaar via <www.icc-pi.int/Menus/ICC/Structure+of+the+Court/Office+of+the+Prosecutor/Comm+and+Ref/ Palestine/> (laatstelijk geraadpleegd op 20 december 2010).

91 Artikel 15 (2) van het Statuut van Rome; Regels 104 en 105 van de *Rules of Procedure and Evidence.*

92 Zie hierover W. Burke-White, 'Implementing a Policy of Positive Complementarity in the Rome System of Justice', *Criminal Law Forum* 2008, p. 61 [hierna: Burke-White, Implementing]; C. Hall, 'Developing and Implementing an Effective Positive Complementarity Prosecution Strategy', in: C. Stahn en G. Sluiter, *The emerging practice of the International Criminal Court*, Leiden: Brill, 2009, p. 220 e.v. [hierna: Hall, Developing].

Ondanks dat sluitend bewijs vooralsnog ontbreekt, lijkt het erop dat het voorlopige onderzoek in Afghanistan heeft bijgedragen aan de daaropvolgende precisering van het luchtaanvalbeleid van de NAVO, en in het bijzonder de Verenigde Staten.[93] De Verenigde Staten lijken ook het belang van interne mechanismes van opsporing en vervolging opnieuw te hebben bevestigd,[94] wat er aan kan hebben bijgedragen dat in april 2010 een militair onderzoek is gestart naar burgerdoden waarvan beweerd werd dat zij door speciale eenheden (special forces) van de VS zouden zijn veroorzaakt.[95]

Op haar beurt werd het voorlopige onderzoek in Irak, dat werd geopend na de ontvangst van verschillende individuele communicaties vanaf 2003, gesloten vanwege de procedures die in het Verenigd Koninkrijk werden gestart naar de oorlogsmisdrijven waarbij Engelse staatsburgers betrokken zouden zijn geweest.[96]

Voorts lijkt het voorlopige onderzoek in Kenia de boodschap van voormalig VN Secretaris-Generaal Kofi Annan, die de Keniaanse autoriteiten waarschuwde dat er geen straffeloosheid voor betrokkenen bij internationale misdrijven zal zijn, te versterken.[97] Wanneer een voorlopig onderzoek onsuccesvol is in het stimuleren van nationale autoriteiten, kan de onderzoeksfase[98] een nuttig mechanisme zijn om het preventieve mandaat van het

---

93 D. Schwammenthal, 'Prosecuting American War Crimes', *The Wall Street Journal*, Den Haag, 26 november 2009, 'Opinion Europe'. Zie ook D. Filkins, 'U.S. Tightens Airstrike Policy in Afghanistan', *The New York Times*, 21 juni 2009, Asia Pacific.

94 Zie E. Barbour en M.C. Weed, 'The International Criminal Court (ICC): Jurisdiction, Extradition, and U.S. Policy', *Congressional Research Service* (16 maart 2010), <assets.opencrs.com/rpts/R41116_20100316.pdf> (laatstelijk geraadpleegd op 20 december 2010), p. 15.

95 Zie L. King, 'Inquiry puts Spotlight on U.S. Special Forces in Afghanistan', *The Los Angeles Times*, Los Angeles, 9 april 2010, waarin wordt verwezen naar het high profile onderzoek in april 2010 naar burgerdoden veroorzaakt door special forces die, tot dat moment, grotendeels uit de publiciteit werden gehouden door het leger van de Verenigde Staten.

96 Zie *Office of the Prosecutor,* 'OTP Response to communications received concerning Iraq' (9 februari 2010), <www.icc-cpi.int/NR/rdonlyres/04D143C8-19FB-466C-AB77 4CDB2FDEBEF7/143682/OTP_letter_to_senders_re_Iraq_9_February_2006.pdf> (laatstelijk geraadpleegd op 20 december 2010), p. 9.

97 Zie het onderzoek van C. Bjork en J. Goebertus, 'Parallel Paths and Unintended Consequences: The Role of Civil Society and the ICC in Rule of Law Strengthening in Kenya', beschikbaar via <works.bepress.com/christine_bjork/1/> (laatstelijk geraadpleegd op 20 december 2010). Zie ook de persverklaring van de Kofi Annan Stichting, met als titel: 'Remarks by Kofi Annan on Conclusion of the Visit to Kenya, 2-8 December 2009', beschikbaar via <kofiannanfoundation.org/newsroom/press/2009/12/remarks-he-kofi-annan-conclusion-visit-to-kenya-au-panel-eminent-african> (laatstelijk geraadpleegd op 20 december 2010). Dit neemt niet weg dat er meer empirisch onderzoek nodig is om met zekerheid uitspraken te kunnen doen over de invloed van voorlopig onderzoek door het Internationaal Strafhof.

98 In deze gevallen kan een kwalitatief onderzoek naar de *gravity threshold* nog steeds de aanvang van een onderzoek rechtvaardigen in situaties waarin internationale misdrijven nog niet zijn gepleegd, of waarin een begin van aanvang is gemaakt. Voor een definitie van een kwalitatief onderzoek naar de *gravity threshold*, zie *Prosecutor v. Abu Garda* (Decision on the Confirmation of Charges) ICC-02/05-02/09 PTC I (8 februari 2010), overwegingen 31-33; *Situation in the Republic of Kenya* (Decision Pursuant to Article 15 of the Rome Statute on the Authorization of an Investigation into the Situation in the Republic of Kenya) ICC-01/09 PTC II (31 maart 2010), overweging 62.

Internationaal Strafhof te vervullen. De Aanklager kan dan immers gebruik maken van dwangmaatregelen[99] en van allerlei vormen van samenwerking met de lidstaten.

Artikel 53 van het Statuut van het Internationaal Strafhof geeft de Aanklager de bevoegdheid om een onderzoek te sluiten indien hij tot de slotsom komt dat er niet voldoende grondslag bestaat voor een vervolging. Deze maatstaf bestaat uit dezelfde criteria die gelden voor een voorlopig onderzoek.[100] Dientengevolge kan de Aanklager een onderzoek sluiten indien dit ertoe heeft geleid dat aarzelende autoriteiten betekenisvolle stappen hebben gezet om de uitvoering van internationale misdrijven (daadwerkelijk) te voorkomen.[101]

IV Tijdige interventie door het Internationaal Strafhof indien internationale misdrijven al plaatsvinden

De tijdige interventie door het Internationaal Strafhof kan ook uitgevoerd worden in situaties waarin al internationale misdrijven worden gepleegd. Het doel in deze situaties is om het plegen van deze internationale misdrijven te beëindigen. Bovendien kan het afzien van toekomstige misdaden niet de aansprakelijkheid voor reeds gepleegde misdaden aantasten. Voorlopige onderzoeken kunnen daarom alleen door de Aanklager worden gestopt op gronden die verband houden met ontvankelijkheid of een goede rechtsbedeling. In deze context gaat het erom nationale autoriteiten te bewegen om het begaan van internationale misdrijven te stoppen[102] alsmede (i) hen aan te sporen tot en hen bij te staan bij het vervullen van hun verplichting om reeds gepleegde internationale misdrijven te onderzoeken en te vervolgen (positieve complementariteit),[103] en (ii) de verantwoordelijkheid om de misdrijven af te doen te delen met het Internationaal Strafhof. Dit vooral in gevallen waarin sprake is van een substantieel capaciteitstekort (coöperatieve comple-

---

99 Zie artikelen 54-57 van het Statuut van Rome.

100 Vergelijk artikel 53 (2) van het Statuut van Rome met artikel 53 (1) van het Statuut van Rome en Regel 48 van de *Rules of Procedure and Evidence*.

101 Bovendien kan de Aanklager, volgens artikel 19 lid 11 van het Statuut van het Internationaal Strafhof, beslissen om het onderzoek op te schorten en toezicht te houden op de ontwikkelingen op nationaal niveau voordat hij het onderzoek formeel sluit.

102 Voor een belangrijk gedeelte lijkt de *Appeals Chamber* van het Internationaal Strafhof hier impliciet zowel een positieve als een coöperatieve complementariteit te hanteren. Zie de beslissing van 22 juni 2009 in de *Katanga en Ngudjolo*-zaak. Zie verder *Prosecutor v Mr Germain Katanga and Mathieu Ngudjolo Chui* (Decision of the Presiding Judge of the Appeals Chamber in the appeal of Germain Katanga against the Decision of Trial Chamber II of 12 June 2009 on the Admissibility of the Case) ICC-01/04-01/07 OA 8 (10 juli 2009).

103 Zie Burke-White, Implementing (voetnoot 92), p. 61 en Hall, Developing (voetnoot 92), p. 220 e.v. Zie ook M.E. Cross en S. Williams, 'Recent Developments at the ICC: Prosecutor v. Germain Katanga and Mathieu Ngudjolo Chui: A Boost for Co-operative Complementarity?', *Human Rights Law Review* 2010, p. 339.

mentariteit).[104] Hieruit volgt dat het ondersteunen van staten bij het versterken van hun juridische systemen en het uitvoeren van nationale procedures een kernelement is van de tijdige interventie door het Internationaal Strafhof.

Zoals uiteengezet is door William Burke-White[105] en Christopher Hall[106] kan de Aanklager gebruikmaken van de hierboven genoemde maatregelen om dit mandaat uit te voeren gedurende zijn voorlopige onderzoek. De Aanklager kan in het bijzonder nationale actoren trainen in het afdoen van internationale misdrijven en hij kan hen begeleiden in het opzetten van veiligheidsprogramma's voor slachtoffers en getuigen en bij het opzetten van effectieve informatiesystemen. Ook kan hij toezicht houden en feedback geven op de ontwikkeling van nationale procedures. Tevens kan hij samenwerken met andere organen van het Internationaal Strafhof om de algemene effectiviteit van preventieve inspanningen te vergroten.

Benadrukt moet worden dat ondanks de internationale samenwerking met andere belanghebbenden, de nationale autoriteiten van ontvangende staten een sterke voorkeur lijken te hebben voor advies van en begeleiding door functionarissen van het Internationaal Strafhof. Omdat nationale autoriteiten zich er bewust van zijn dat hun inspanningen om internationale misdrijven te voorkomen, beoordeeld zullen worden door het Internationaal Strafhof, worden het advies en de begeleiding van het Internationaal Strafhof als uiterst belangrijk beschouwd voor het succes van die inspanningen. Als gevolg daarvan is het potentieel van het Internationaal Strafhof om door middel van tijdige interventie de rechtsstaat en beginselen van goed bestuur te versterken erg groot.[107] Het voorlopige onderzoek in Colombia geeft enige indicaties van dit potentieel.

---

104 A. Cassese e.a., 'The Rome Statute: A Tentative Assessment', in: A. Cassese e.a. (red.), *The Rome Statute of the International Criminal Court: A Commentary,* Oxford: OUP, 2002, p. 1906; Kress, '"Self-Referrals" and "Waivers of Complementarity": Some Considerations in Law and Policy', *Journal of International Criminal Justice* 2004, p. 947-948; en F. Gioia, 'State Sovereignty, Jurisdiction, and "Modern" International Law: The Principle of Complementarity in the International Criminal Court', *Leiden Journal of International Law* 2006 1095, p. 1115.

105 Burke-White, Implementing (voetnoot 92), p. 61.

106 Hall, Developing (voetnoot 92), p. 220 e.v.

107 Zie hierover ook: W. Burke-White, 'Complementarity in Practice: The International Criminal Court as Part of a System of Multi-level Global Governance in the Democratic Republic of Congo', *Leiden Journal of International Law* 2005, p. 589-590. Op het herzieningscongres betreffende het Internationaal Strafhof is in juni 2010 door het *stocktaking bureau* een voorstel gedaan met betrekking tot het complementariteitsbeginsel. Het Secretariaat van de Vergadering van Staten die Partij zijn bij het Statuut zou de taak moeten krijgen om de informatieuitwisseling tussen het Hof, de staten die partij zijn, de staten die het Statuut hebben getekend, internationale organisaties, het maatschappelijk middenveld en andere betrokkenen te vergemakkelijken met als doel het versterken van de positie van nationale jurisdicties (Report of the Stocktaking Report on the Principle of Complementarity, 'Taking Stock of the Principle of Complementarity: Bridging the Impunity Gap' (18 maart 2010) ICC-ASP/8/51, overweging 54 (e)). Hoewel dit voorstel een eerste stap in de goede richting kan zijn, is het nog onvoldoende, gezien de mogelijkheden die er zijn om de rechtsstaat en behoorlijk bestuur te versterken in ontvangende staten door middel van tijdige interventie.

Pas in mei 2006 begonnen de onderzoeken naar de sinds 2003[108] gedemobiliseerde paramilitairen, toen het constitutionele hof het belangrijkste onderdeel van het demobilisatieproces handhaafde: 'de Vrede en Rechtvaardigheidswet'.[109] Snel daarna maakte de Aanklager van het Internationaal Strafhof zijn voorlopige onderzoek bekend[110] en in oktober 2007 en augustus 2008 bracht hij twee persoonlijke bezoeken aan Colombia.[111]

Sindsdien heeft het Hooggerechtshof van Colombia het belang onderstreept dat onderzoeken onder 'de Vrede en Rechtvaardigheidswet' zich concentreren op (i) het patroon van internationale misdrijven die gepleegd zijn jegens de bevolking en (ii) de structuur, het lidmaatschap en de externe steun van de paramilitaire organisatie die de misdaden heeft begaan.[112] Dit heeft zijn weerslag gevonden in het zestien pagina's tellende protocol voor het presenteren van bewijs, zoals uitgevaardigd op 23 augustus 2010 door de raadkamer van het Hof voor Vrede en Rechtvaardigheid in Bogota.

Bovendien voert het Colombiaanse Hooggerechtshof sinds het einde van 2007 onderzoeken uit en stelt het vervolgingen in naar één derde van de leden van het Colombiaanse parlement[113] en negentien senatoren[114] wegens mogelijke banden met paramilitaire groepen. Deze procedures, die gebaseerd zijn op bekentenissen van gedemobiliseerde paramilitaire leiders, hebben tot nu toe tot achttien veroordelingen geleid, vooral van leden van de politieke partij die de Colombiaanse regering in 2007 steunde. Deze bekentenissen hebben ook geleid tot het onderzoek naar honderd ambtenaren, lokale politici en leden van de gewapende macht en de politie in de lagere rechtbanken.[115]

Het staat vast dat slechts een handvol hooggeplaatste militairen en politieambtenaren onderworpen zijn aan een onderzoek, en dat de toepassing van 'de Vrede en Rechtvaardigheidswet' zich geconfronteerd ziet met

108 Het demobilisatieproces is het gevolg van het Akkoord van Santa Fé, dat op 15 juli 2003 werd ondertekend door de Colombiaanse regering en de zogenoemde *Autodefensas Unidas de Colombian* (AUC).

109 Zie de uitspraak van het Colombiaanse Constitutionele Hof van 18 mei 2006, C-370/ 2006. Zie ook J.E. Arvelo, 'International Law and Conflict Resolution in Colombia: Balancing Peace and Justice in the Paramilitary Demobilization Process', *Georgetown Journal of International Law* 2006, p. 411-476.

110 Zie Internationaal Strafhof, 'Colombia' <www.icc-cpi.int/Menus/ICC/Structure+of+the+Court/Office+of+the+Prosecutor/Comm+and+Ref/Colombia> (laatstelijk geraadpleegd op 20 december 2010).

111 Idem.

112 Zie onder andere de hoger beroepszaken van de Strafkamer van het Colombiaanse Hooggerechtshof in de zaken (i) Wilson Salazar Carrascal (a.k.a. *el loro*), zaaknr. 31539 (31 juli 2009); en (ii) Gian Carlos Gutierrez Suarez (a.k.a. *el tuerto*), zaaknr. 32022 (21 september 2009).

113 Onderzoek is ingesteld tegen 46 van de 102 leden van de Senaat en tegen 39 van de 166 leden van de Kamer van Afgevaardigden. Zie de informatie die Verdad Abierta tot juli 2010 heeft verzameld die verwijst naar data die door de Rainbow Foundation beschikbaar is gesteld, <www.verdadabierta.com/reconstruyendo/1856-estadisticas>.

114 Idem.

115 Idem.

significante uitdagingen zoals (i) het gebrek aan openbaarheid van de selectiecriteria voor de gedemobiliseerde paramilitaire leden die onder die wet worden onderzocht, (ii) het lage aantal veroordelingen tot dusver; (iii) de uitlevering van veertien hooggeplaatste paramilitaire leiders aan de Verenigde Staten op grond van verdenking van drugshandel; (iv) het gebrek aan demobilisatie van guerrillaleden; (v) de nieuwe toename in het gebruik van geweld, onder andere aangespoord door gewapende groepen bestaande uit vroegere paramilitaire leden.[116]

Niettemin moet men bij het beoordelen van de bijdrage die de procedures voor internationale misdrijven in Colombia leveren aan het versterken van de rechtsstaat en het bevorderen van goed bestuur, rekening houden met het feit dat paramilitaire groepen en hun handlangers decennialang straffeloosheid genoten in Colombia.

Zoals de bezoeken van de Colombiaanse hoofdaanklager en een grote delegatie van het Colombiaanse Hooggerechtshof aan het Internationaal Strafhof in 2010 ons hebben laten zien, lijkt het voorlopige onderzoek van de Aanklager bij te dragen aan de nieuwe situatie in Colombia. Toch is het moeilijk om die invloed op de nationale Colombiaanse autoriteiten te meten, aangezien er verschillende andere factoren zijn die ook bijdragen, zoals: (i) de voorwaarden die het Amerikaanse Congres heeft gesteld voor Amerikaanse militaire hulp en gunstige handelsvoorwaarden voor Colombia;[117] en (ii) de veroordelingen van het Inter-Amerikaans Hof voor de Mensenrechten

---

116 Zie voor een algemene analyse van het proces aangaande vrede en rechtvaardigheid: K. Ambos, *Procedimiento de La Ley de Justicia y Paz (Ley de 2005) y Derecho Penal Internacional*, Bogotá: GTZ, Universidad de Göttingen, 2010; Comisión Colombiana de Juristas, *Anotaciones sobre la Ley de Justicia y Paz: Una Mirada desde los Derechos de las Víctimas*, Bogotá, Comisión Colombiana de Juristas, 2007. Zie ook de recente publicatie van professor Kai Ambos, die hij geschreven heeft in de context van het rondetafelgesprek in Den Haag met non-gouvernementele organisaties over de situatie in Colombia, georganiseerd door het Internationaal Strafhof op 19 en 20 oktober 2010: K. Ambos, F. Huber, 'The Colombian Peace Process and the Principle of Complementarity of the International Criminal Court: Is there sufficient willingness and ability on the part of the Colombian authorities or should the Prosecutor open an investigation now?', 5 januari 2011, <www.icc-cpi.int/NR/rdonlyres/2770C2C8-309A-408E-A41B-0E69F098F421/282850/civil1.pdf>.

117 De definitieve verklaring van het Amerikaanse ministerie van Buitenlandse Zaken betreffende de Colombiaanse strijdkrachten en de door de Verenigde Staten gestelde voorwaarden over de eerbiediging van de mensenrechten, vond plaats op 9 september 2010. Zie hierover: United States Embassy in Bogotá, 'Resolución y Certificación del Gobierno Colombiano y de las Fuerzas Armadas con respect a los Condicionamientos en Derechos Humanos' (15 september 2010) <spanish.bogota.usembassy.gov/pr_117_15092010.html>. Het rapport van de Amerikaanse 'State Department' kan ook gevonden worden op de website van de 'Colombian Commission of Jurists'. Het rapport onderzoekt tot in detail of de Colombiaanse strijdkrachten zich in 2009 hebben gedragen conform de mensenrechtenvoorwaarden zoals die door de Amerikaanse Senaat zijn gesteld (US Department of State, 'Memorandum of Justification concerning Human Rights Conditions with respect to Assistance for the Colombian Armed Forces' (september 2010) <www.coljuristas.org/ LinkClick.aspx?fileticket=ksYH5X9Cvy0%3d&tabid=160&language=es-CO>).

vanwege paramilitair geweld.[118] In deze context zal een verdere coördinatie van tijdige interventie door het Internationaal Strafhof en deze andere actoren de effectiviteit van maatregelen die conform/ingevolge de notie van verantwoordelijkheid om te beschermen door de internationale gemeenschap zijn opgelegd, vergroten.

In dit opzicht moet opgemerkt worden dat de behoefte tot verdere coördinatie tussen de Verenigde Naties en het Internationaal Strafhof bijzonder dringend is,[119] vooral in het licht van zowel hun wederzijdse erkenning als hun inzet om samen te werken,[120] als de bestaande waarborgen tegen bemoeienis van het Internationaal Strafhof met de rol van de Veiligheidsraad.[121]

---

118 Zie de uitspraken van het Inter-Amerikaans Hof voor Mensenrechten in de zaak *19 Comerciantes v. Colombia*, Serie C, 93 (5 juli 2004); de zaak aangaande de slachting bij Mapiripán v. Colombia, Serie C, 122 (15 september 2005); de zaak aangaande de slachting bij Pueblo Bello v. Colombia, Serie C, 140 (31 januari 2006); zaak aangaande de slachting bij Ituango, Serie C, 148 (1 juli 2006); en de zaak Manuel Cepeda Vargas v. Colombia, Serie C, 213 (26 mei 2010).

119 A. Cassese, 'Is the ICC Still Having Teething Problems', *Journal of International Criminal Justice* 2006, p. 436. Zie ook N. Jain, 'A Separate Law for Peacekeepers: The Clash between the Security Council and the International Criminal Court', *European Journal of International Law* 2005, p. 239-254.

120 Overwegingen 7 en 9 van de Preambule van het Statuut van het Internationaal Strafhof bevestigen de doelen en de beginselen van het Handvest van de Verenigde Naties en benadrukken de wil van de lidstaten om het Internationaal Strafhof op te richten in overeenstemming met het VN-systeem. Bovendien staat artikel 87 (7) van het Statuut het het Internationaal Strafhof toe om een geconstateerd gebrek aan medewerking van staten ter overweging naar de VN Veiligheidsraad te sturen. Andere bepalingen, zoals artikel 87 (6) van het Statuut van het Internationaal Strafhof, bepalen dat het Internationaal Strafhof bevoegd is elke intergouvernementele organisatie te verzoeken informatie of documenten te verstrekken, en om andere vormen van samenwerking en rechtshulp te verzoeken die worden overeengekomen met een dergelijke organisatie en in overeenstemming zijn met haar bevoegdheid of mandaat. Bovendien bepaalt artikel 115 van het Statuut van Rome dat de kosten van het Hof en de Vergadering van Staten die Partij zijn gefinancierd kunnen worden door 'fondsen verschaft door de Verenigde Naties, afhankelijk van de goedkeuring van de Algemene Vergadering, in het bijzonder met betrekking tot de kosten die zijn gemaakt ten gevolge van aangiften door de Veiligheidsraad.' Op haar beurt is de 'Negotiated Relationship Agreement between the ICC and the United Nations' (vastgesteld ingevolge artikel 2 van het Statuut van het Internationaal Strafhof) gebaseerd op wederzijdse erkenning tussen de VN en het Internationaal Strafhof en op een belofte tot samenwerking. In de preambule bij deze overeenkomst wordt 'the important role assigned to the International Criminal Court in dealing with the most serious crimes of concern to the international community as a whole [...] and which threaten the peace, security and well-being of the world' benadrukt. De genoemde overeenkomst weidt, op basis van een algemene verplichting van wederzijdse erkenning, coördinatie en overleg zoals neergelegd in artikel 3, uit over de modaliteiten van samenwerking tussen de twee organisaties zoals de verwijzingen door de VN Veiligheidsraad (artikel 17(1) van de Negotiated Relationship Agreement), de verzoeken door de VN Veiligheidsraad tot schorsing van onderzoeken en vervolgingen door het Internationaal Strafhof, (artikel 17(2) van de Negotiated Relationship Agreement), de samenwerking door de VN Veiligheidsraad onder voorwaarde van vertrouwelijkheid (artikel 18(3) van de Negotiated Relationship Agreement), en samenwerking door de VN Veiligheidsraad met de Aanklager van het Internationaal Strafhof in het kader van voorlopig onderzoek (artikel 18(2) van de Negotiated Relationship Agreement).

121 De artikelen 12, 13 en 16 van het Statuut van het Internationaal Strafhof stellen de VN Veiligheidsraad in staat om alle situaties die zich na 1 juli 2002 hebben voorgedaan bij het Internationaal Strafhof aan te geven zonder beperking van jurisdictie, en om het Internationaal Strafhof te verzoeken onderzoek of vervolging op te schorten voor een periode van 12 maanden. Bovendien

V Conclusie

Het preventieve mandaat van het Internationaal Strafhof is een belangrijk middel om de verantwoordelijkheid die de internationale gemeenschap heeft conform de notie van verantwoordelijkheid om te beschermen, te vervullen. Tot nu toe heeft de focus vooral gelegen op inspanningen van het Internationaal Strafhof ten behoeve van generale preventie door straffeloosheid uit te bannen voor reeds gepleegde internationale misdrijven. Toch is de bijdrage die het Internationaal Strafhof kan leveren aan het voorkomen van toekomstige internationale misdrijven door middel van tijdige interventie, in potentie nog groter.

Om dit potentieel te verwezenlijken moet de preventieve rol van het Internationaal Strafhof door middel van tijdige interventies worden erkend door de verschillende organen van het Hof. Ook is vereist dat de lidstaten deze rol erkennen, zodat zij de nodige middelen beschikbaar zullen stellen en strafrechtelijke aansprakelijkheid vestigen voor het plannen en voorbereiden van alle internationale misdrijven. Als aan deze premissen is voldaan zal verdere coördinatie tussen het Internationaal Strafhof, de Verenigde Naties en andere belanghebbenden het preventieve effect van hun tijdige interventie bevorderen. Wat uiteindelijk van belang is, is of het Internationaal Strafhof één van de verschillende mechanismes blijft voor het vestigen van aansprakelijkheid met een beperkt generaal preventief mandaat, of dat het in plaats daarvan zijn potentieel verwezenlijkt om door middel van tijdige intreventie internationale misdrijven te voorkomen, de rechtsstaat te versterken en behoorlijk bestuur te bevorderen.

Dankwoord

Graag bedank ik de Rector Magnificus en de Raad van Bestuur van de Universiteit Utrecht voor mijn benoeming als hoogleraar international straf(proces)recht. Mijn dank gaat ook uit naar het bestuur van de faculteit Recht, Economie, Bestuur en Organisatie, en in het bijzonder naar het departement Rechtsgeleerdheid voor het vertrouwen dat in mij gesteld is door mijn

---

heeft de Vergadering van Staten die Partij zijn onlangs tijdens het eerste Herzieningscongres unaniem besloten dat het Internationaal Strafhof zijn jurisdictie over het misdrijf agressie slechts zal uitoefenen nadat het heeft geverifieerd of de VN Veiligheidsraad een daad van agressie van de betreffende staat heeft vastgesteld. Zonder een dergelijke verklaring kan het Internationaal Strafhof haar handelingen slechts voortzetten indien het handelt op basis van een verwijzing door een lidstaat of een individuele communicatie, en indien de plenaire vergadering van de 'Pre-Trial Division' hiertoe toestemming geeft (zie Annex I to Resolution RC/Res.6 (11 juni 2010) getiteld 'Amendments to the Rome Statute of the International Criminal Court on the Crime of Agression', artikel 15 bis, lid 6).

benoeming te steunen. Ik zal mijn uiterste best te doen om aan deze verwachtingen te voldoen.

Graag bedank ik ook het Willem Pompe Instituut, het Internationaal Strafhof en het ICTY. In het bijzonder bedank ik graag Sylvia Steiner, al bijna een decennium mijn baas en goede vriendin. Ik zal haar nooit vergeten.

Graag betuig ik mijn erkentelijkheid aan ambassadeur Juan Antonio Yañez-Barnuevo, professor Maria del Carmen Calvo, William Fenrick en Pieter Kruger voor het vertrouwen in mij tien jaar geleden, toen niemand vertrouwen in mij had. Ook betuig ik graag van mijn dankbaarheid jegens mijn collega's hier in Utrecht, die hun vertrouwen hebben gesteld in een jonge Spaanse professor met een 'piratenaccent'; John, Ige, Stijn, François, Dina, Chrisje, Annemarieke, Leo, Eric, Diana, Enrique, Jill en Dessy – heel erg bedankt.

A mis padres Valentín y Mercedes quiero agradecerles el amor y el apoyo desinteresado que siempre me han ofrecido desde el día en que, gracias a ellos, vi la luz por primera vez. Ellos son, sin duda, los verdaderos responsables de aquello que soy hoy.

Ook bedank ik graag mijn zusters Laura en Ana, die gisteren vanuit Spanje zijn gereisd om hier vandaag bij te kunnen zijn. In het bijzonder ben ik Laura veel dank verschuldigd voor haar loyaliteit in de moeilijkste tijden en aan mijn andere broers en zusters, Pablo José en Elena, die hier vandaag helaas niet bij kunnen zijn. Ik wens hen geluk en blijdschap toe.

Graag bedank ik Gordon Brandt, voor zijn onschatbare hulp in het voorbereiden van deze presentatie, en Sonia, Edwin, Julian, Ana Maria, Alejandro, Romina, Julieta, Teresa en Salvador, die mij altijd gesteund hebben, ook in de moeilijkste situaties. In het bijzonder nog enkele woorden van hoop en steun voor Sonia, die momenteel ernstige, maar niet onoverwinnelijke, gezondheidsproblemen heeft.

En natuurlijk bedank ik ook nog graag Paola, die de afgelopen anderhalf jaar dagelijks heeft moeten lijden als gevolg van de totstandkoming van deze rede, en dankzij wie ik weer in de liefde ben gaan geloven. Ik heb maar twee woorden voor haar: 'Te quiero'.

Tot slot wil ik aan iedereen die hier op deze onvergetelijke dag aanwezig is mijn meest oprechte dank betuigen voor uw aanwezigheid.

Daarmee sluit ik deze rede af door, naar het advies van Gerda Blok en Carin Schnitger, te zeggen 'Ik heb gezegd'.

1. *Facetten van economisch strafrecht*, prof. jhr. mr. M. Wladimiroff (red.), 1990
2. *Buiten de muren*, dr. mr. M. Moerings en mr. G. ter Haar (red.), 1990
3. *De sociale constructie van fraude*, dr. C.H. Brants en dr. K.L.K. Brants, 1991
4. *Om de persoon van de dader*, dr. J.A. Janse de Jonge, 1991
5. *Ziek of schuldig?*, drs. F. Koenraadt (red.), 1991
6. *In de bisnis*, Sari van der Poel, 1991
7. *Strafrechtelijke handhaving van gemeenschapsrecht*, mr. R.M.A. Guldenmund, 1992
8. *Homoseksualiteit en recht*, dr. mr. M. Moerings en mr. A. Mattijssen (red.), 1992
9. *Met schuld beladen*, dr. J.A. Janse de Jonge en prof. mr. C. Kelk (red.), 1992
10. *Binnen de steen van dit bestaan*, J.A. Janse de Jonge, M. Moerings en A. van Vliet (red.), 1993
11. *Strafrecht en milieu*, dr. Th.J.B. Buiting, 1993
12. *Latijnsamerikaanse drugkoeriersters in detentie: ezels of zondebokken?*, Janine Jansen, 1994
13. *De overdracht van de tenuitvoerlegging van strafvonnissen*, D.J.M.W. Paridaens, 1994
14. *Hoe punitief is Nederland?*, dr. mr. M. Moerings (eindred.), 1994
15. *Buitenlandse getuigen in strafzaken*, André Klip, 1994
16. *De menselijke verantwoordelijkheid in het strafrecht*, prof. mr. C. Kelk, 1994
17. *De naam van het feit*, C.M. Pelser, 1995
18. *Allah, Satan en het recht*, Yücel Yeşilgöz, 1995
19. *Een schijn van kans*, M. Gras, F. Bovenkerk, K. Gorter, P. Kruiswijk en D. Ramsoedt, 1996
20. *Er is meer*, C.H. Brants, C. Kelk en M. Moerings (red.), 1996
21. *Ouderdoding als ultiem delict*, F. Koenraadt, 1996
22. *Bedreigde getuigen in het strafproces*, Annemarieke Beijer, 1997
23. *Politie en criminaliteit van Marokkaanse jongens*, Rosan Coppes, Flora de Groot en Alex Sheerazi, 1997
24. *Locus delicti en rechtsmacht*, H.D. Wolswijk, 1998
25. *Voorwaarden voor strafbaarstelling van vrouwenhandel*, Roelof Haveman, 1998
26. *Met recht behoorlijk ingesloten*, Anje Brouwer, 1998
27. *Over levende gedachten*, C.H. Brants, 1999
28. *Morele kwesties in het strafrecht*, M. Moerings, C.M. Pelser en C.H. Brants (red.), 1999
29. *Eerlijke berechting en bijzonder straf(proces)recht*, P.J. Baauw, 1999
30. *Decentraal bestuur vervolgbaar?*, J.A.E. van der Jagt, 2000
31. *Recht voor commuun gestraften*, Miranda Boone, 2000
32. *Misdaadvermogen en internationaal strafrecht*, Roan Lamp, 2000
33. *Nederlands detentierecht*, prof. mr. C. Kelk, 2000
34. *De Wet Terwee*, Renée Kool en Martin Moerings, 2001
35. *De Penitentiaire Beginselenwet in werking*, M. Boone en G. de Jonge (red.), 2001
36. *Opsporing van oorlogsmisdrijven*, A. Beijer, A.H. Klip, M.A. Oomen en A.M.J. van der Spek, 2002
37. *Recht op schrift*, dr. Renée Kool, prof. dr. Martin Moerings en Willem Zandbergen, 2002

38. *Herstelrecht in jeugdstrafzaken*, Ytje Minke Hokwerda, 2004
39. *Voor wat hoort wat: plea bargaining in het strafrecht*, Chrisje Brants en Bart Stapert, 2004
40. *Het psychisch onvermogen terecht te staan*, Peter Bal en Frans Koenraadt, 2004
41. *Discretie in het strafrecht*, M. Boone, R.S.B. Kool, C.M. Pelser en T. Boekhout van Solinge (red.), 2004
42. *Dealing with Drugs in Europe*, Tim Boekhout van Solinge, 2004
43. *Voor de vorm*, A.A. Franken, 2004
44. *Detentie en culturele diversiteit*, Marieke Post, 2005
45. *Multiculturaliteit en verdediging in strafzaken*, Mirjam Siesling, 2006
46. *Strafbare discriminatie*, Chrisje Brants, Renée Kool en Allard Ringnalda, 2007
47. *Externe openbaarheid in het strafproces*, Leonie van Lent, 2008
48. *De centrale positie van grensgevallen*, Frans Koenraadt, 2008
49. *Strafrecht binnen menselijke proporties*, Constantijn Kelk, 2008
50. *Constante waarden*, A.A. Franken, M. de Langen en M. Moerings (red.), 2008
51. *Meningen van gedetineerden – vijftig jaar later*, M. Moerings, M. Boone en A.A. Franken, 2008
52. *Gedachten van Willem Pompe over de mens in het strafrecht*, 2008
53. *De tenuitvoerlegging van sancties: maatwerk door de rechter?* M. Boone, A. Beijer, A.A. Franken en C. Kelk, 2009
54. *Strafrechtelijke causaliteit*, F.G.H. Kristen, 2009
55. *Vrijheid en verlangen*, F. Koenraadt en I. Weijers (red.), 2009
56. *Diverse kwesties*, Chrisje Brants en Sari van der Poel (red.), 2009
57. *Etniciteit, criminaliteit en het strafrecht*, Frank Bovenkerk, 2009
58. *Prudentie en evidentie*, Antoine Mooij, 2009
59. *Balanceren met recht*, D. van der Hoeven, K. Eppink, F. Koenraadt en M. Boone, 2009
60. *Daad-Schuld*, Ferry de Jong, 2009
61. *De aantrekkingskracht van 'gevaarlijke' mannen*, Marion van San, 2010
62. *Maffia, diamanten en Mozart*, Dina Siegel, 2010
63. *Subjectiviteit in strafrecht en psychiatrie*, Frans Koenraadt (red.), 2010
64. *Het verlof van de ter beschikking gestelde*, F. Koenraadt, Ph.M. Langbroek, J. Tigchelaar en E.G. van der Velde, 2010
65. *Bijzonder strafrecht*, F.G.H. Kristen, R.M.I. Lamp, J.M.W. Lindeman en M.J.J.P. Luchtman, 2011
66. *Papieren werkelijkheid*, Petra van Kampen, 2011
67. *Homo ludens en humaan strafrecht*, Frans Koenraadt en Ria Wolleswinkel (red.), 2011
68. *De rol van het Internationaal Strafhof in het voorkomen van internationale misdrijven door middel van tijdige interventie*, Hector Olásolo, 2011

De delen 1-37 zijn verschenen bij Gouda Quint / Kluwer Juridische uitgevers, Deventer. Vanaf deel 38 verschijnt de Pompe-reeks bij Boom Lemma uitgevers, Den Haag. Bestellingen: Boom distributiecentrum, Postbus 400, 7940 AK Meppel, tel. 0522-237555, fax 0522-253864, e-mail: budh@boomdistributiecentrum.nl.